Follow Your True Colors
To The Work You Love

The Popular Method for Matching Your Personality to Your Career

Carolyn Kalil

True Colors, Inc. Publishing
Santa Ana, California

Copyright 1998 by Carolyn Kalil
Second Printing 1999
Third Printing 2000
Fourth Printing 2000
Fifth Printing 2001
Sixth Printing 2002
Seventh Printing 2004
Eighth Printing 2005
All rights reserved
Printed in the United States of America by Offset Solutions
Library of Congress Catalog 97-78111
New ISBN 1-893320-28-6
Former ISBN 1-885221-94-0

True Colors, Inc. Publishing

3605 W. MacArthur Blvd. #702
Santa Ana, CA 92704

TCP218-A

To my dad, my first hero

Acknowledgments

Giving birth to this book has truly been a profound labor of love which I could not have accomplished alone. I would like to express my sincere gratitude to the following people who have made a contribution to this effort:

My publishers, Thorn and Ursula Bacon, for recognizing the value in spreading the True Colors message.

My editor, Dave Lindstedt, who put his heart and soul into my manuscript.

My husband, Emil, for believing in me and teaching me computer skills.

The creator of True Colors, Don Lowry, for his vision and the gift of True Colors.

My personal coach, Joseph Murphy, for his love and support in helping me overcome many of the obstacles in completing this book.

My spiritual teacher, Reverend Michael Beckwith, who taught me the practical use of spiritual principles.

My soul-buddy, Carol Imai, for taking the True Colors journey with me from the beginning.

My intuitive friend, Susan, who saw the vision for this book long before its completion.

Oprah Winfrey, who I've never met but is nevertheless my role model for her wisdom and courage to show her true colors to the world.

Table of Contents

Prologue

When I was in the second grade, one day the teacher asked the class to line up according to eye color: blue eyes in this line and brown eyes over there. My eyes are one of those 'tweener colors, more green than blue, but not quite either, with yellow flecks just to keep you guessing. I was a precocious and precise little kid, so I asked the obvious question: "What about green eyes?" I'll never forget my teacher's response: "There's no such thing as green eyes; your eyes are blue, get in the blue-eyed line."

You know as well as I do that eyes come in more than two colors, but it wasn't until I read the book you are now holding that I realized personalities come in a variety of colors as well. Don't misunderstand, I knew people were different, but every system I had seen for describing those differences boiled down to an alphabet soup that I could never quite keep straight. Whether I was an INTJ or an ESPN didn't seem to have any practical application.

At work, it often appeared that my personality got in the way, and even though I achieved some financial success through hard work and determination, I didn't quite fit the jobs I was trying to do. I was frustrated. Too bad this book wasn't written back then.

Eventually I met a wise career counselor who showed me that for years I had been a green-eyed guy standing in a blue-eyed line, doing work that didn't match my natural gifts, interests and abilities. He explained that it takes two elements to achieve job satisfaction: *what* you do, and *where* you do it. With more than 60,000 career classifications in the United States, spread across untold thousands of organizations, you're bound to find a pretty close fit somewhere if you know what you're looking for.

But how can you know?

The first step is to understand who you are and how you are wired, because your true colors are as natural a part of you as the color of your eyes. I can now see that the very characteristics that were evident in me way back in the second grade — attention to detail, precise language, and inquisitiveness — all fit my calling as a book editor. One of the joys of my newfound profession is the opportunity to work with true-blue authors like Carolyn Kalil.

As you will soon see, the True Colors™ system is easy to understand, fun to work with, and insightful. It will start you on the road to discovering how your true colors fit in the spectrum of opportunities that lie before you. Don't waste another minute. Turn the page and get started!

Dave Lindstedt, Editor

Introduction

‹ ‹ ‹ ‹ ‹ ‹ ‹ ‹ ‹ ‹ ‹ ‹ ‹ › › › › › › › › › › › › ›

Several years ago when I began to write this book, a very intuitive friend of mine told me, "The book you're going to write is not the book you think you're going to write." At the time I had no clue what she meant by her uncanny remark. But she was right. The book you now hold in your hands is certainly different from the one I set out to write. My initial intent was to introduce cutting-edge information about a simple personality system that helps people understand who they are. This knowledge became the catalyst for my own mental, spiritual and emotional healing, which gave me the courage to discover and pursue the work I love to do. This book is based on my personal experience and insights, as well as feedback from some whom I have counseled.

In my early days as a college career counselor, when students would ask me to help them find the work they should do, I would take them literally. It didn't take long to realize they were really asking much deeper questions, such as, Who am I? Why am I here? What is the purpose of my life? What was I born to do? Where do I fit?

Many fine books already on the market deal with the nuts and bolts of the job-hunting process, how to write a résumé, how to interview, and where to find particular kinds of work. My focus differs by first tackling the age-old issues of knowing who we are and our purpose — internal issues of self-discovery and meaning — before applying that knowledge to the task of finding our ideal life's work.

For as long as I can remember, I have been able to see the natural potential in others, but for years I didn't have a name for it. I was frustrated because I didn't know how to explain to other people what I knew. Still, it was clear to me that innate qualities in individuals motivated them to think and behave in particular ways. Everyone has unique and special characteristics that have nothing to do with one's race, religion or level of education.

Why is it that some people have the incredible ability to connect and interact easily with other people, while many do not have this gift, yet possess remarkably curious minds that are storehouses for a wealth of information? Why are some people gung-ho for life without worrying how they're going to get where they're going or what will happen when they arrive, while others seem almost paralyzed without first developing a detailed plan to get from point A to point B?

As a counselor, I have discovered a way to show others what these traits are and how to use them to find their own unique niche that brings them satisfaction in their work.

In 1988, I discovered the True Colors Personality System™ and began to use it in career counseling to identify the natural potential in people. True Colors™ was designed in 1979 by Don Lowry, combining four colors with four distinct personality types. He presented his program as a stage production with actors playing the roles of the four personalities.

I became a trainer for True Colors, teaching many professionals and non-professionals in the United States and Canada how to use this system. In 1989, Don Lowry and I co-authored a workbook, *How to Express Your Natural Skills and Talents in A Career*, which integrates the True Colors Personality System into the career decision-making process.

As a career counselor, I had long encouraged others to choose work that would bring out their passion. With True Colors, I now had a tool to show them how to do this. My college career-planning classes became very popular as students not only figured out what they wanted to do with their lives but also understood themselves and their relationships better than ever.

My personal and professional success with True Colors inspired me to write this book. It spoke to my heart like no other personality system had ever done and I knew I was on to something good that could change lives.

Classifying individuals according to four main personality types is not a new idea. The eminent physician Hippocrates described four dispositions or temperaments — choleric, phlegmatic, melancholic and sanguine — as long ago as the fifth century B.C. Eastern astrologers devised a system that used four natural elements, air, water, earth and fire, to create the trigons that comprise the twelve signs of the zodiac. Native Americans divide their medicine wheel into four Spirit Keepers, and the four central desires of Hindu philosophy—pleasure, success, duty and meaning—delineate four aspects of human nature.

In the modern era, Carl Jung's landmark work *Psychological Types* reaffirms the ancient belief in fixed patterns of behavior. According to Jung, each of us is born with a particular basic personality and our goal is not to be like anyone else, but to become our "best self." Despite its powerful influence, Jung's typology was not adaptable to everyday use until the relatively recent development of the Myers-Briggs Type Indicator, which sparked a renewed interest in personality theory.

Modern-day psychologist Dr. David Keirsey, in his book *Please Understand Me*, explains the relationship between the four temperaments and the sixteen Myers-Briggs Types. Keirsey labels the four temperaments the Apollonian, the Promethean, the Epimethean, and the Dionysian.

The genius of Don Lowry was to simplify further the language used to discuss personality and replace the complicated labels with simple colors: blue, green, gold and orange. Suddenly, what had been a complex information system available only to professionals was now easily understood and used by anyone.

You are about to embark on an incredibly exciting journey. Through the True Colors process you will uncover your positive attributes and learn how they already suit you for work you will love to do. Once you have recognized your true colors, you'll understand why some careers are natural extensions of who you are, while others will never fit — and in fact, might harm your spiritual and emotional well-being. The final steps in this process are to help you overcome your fear, define your mission, and set your course for expressing your true self through a meaningful life's work.

1

Who Am I?

‹ ‹ ‹ ‹ ‹ ‹ ‹ ‹ ‹ ‹ ‹ ‹ › › › › › › › › › › › ›

The truly extraordinary thing about the truth is that whenever you hear it you know instantly that you have always known it. Discovery is a process of remembering.

Alegra Taylor

As a child, I loved talking, listening, and interacting with others. I was popular among friends at school, at church and in my own neighborhood. People seemed to gravitate to me and I genuinely enjoyed communicating with them. I was sensitive to other people's feelings and intuitively knew how to say the right things to make them feel better. When other kids were hurting, I would be the first to come to their rescue, sometimes even crying with them over their problems. Because I was mature for my age, I could talk to adults as easily as other children. Grown-ups treated me more like a peer than a child and often told me about their problems.

I recently learned that my mother used me as a sounding board when I was only three years old. When something was bothering her she would take me for long walks and talk to me about her problems. We'd stop for a soda and I would look at her as though I totally understood, pat her on the back and say, "Everything will be all right, mother baby." She said she actually believed me and would feel better. Obviously, these personality traits were evident early in my life but I had no idea they would be the very natural strengths and talents that would lead me to the work I love.

Growing up in Salt Lake City, Utah, I can remember being in the fifth grade and pretending to be listening to my teacher. I had a tendency to daydream a lot, and on one particular day, I was staring out the window, asking myself, Who am I? Why am I here? What is the meaning of life? I had asked myself these questions before but had never uttered these words to anyone, fearing they would think I was strange or weird. I even thought maybe I was the only one ever to ponder these thoughts because I had never heard anyone discuss them. I just kept hoping and praying that without asking, somebody — anybody — would see the real me and give me the answers to these questions.

Although I was very confused about who I was, I knew I couldn't look to my own family to help me figure it out. The eldest of six girls, instead of feeling close to any of my sisters, I acted more like a surrogate parent. My father and I have similar personality traits and he was the only one to whom I truly felt connected. Smart, handsome and charming, my dad was often the center of attention and admired by most people who knew him. Unfortunately, I seldom saw my dad. He and my mother separated early in my life and my father moved to another state.

My mother, on the other hand, was different from my father and me. She was a very beautiful yet modest woman with a more reserved, practical and serious nature. If opposites attract, this was certainly true in the case of my mother and father. My mother's main concern was meeting our survival needs for enough food on the table and a roof over our heads. Accomplishing that, she focused on disciplining us, keeping us and our house neat and clean, and making sure we went to school on time. She believed that children should be seen and not heard.

Raising six children and working, she had little time to pay attention to any of us as individuals.

My mother took much pride in saying, "I treat all my kids the same." She didn't believe in making a fuss or in treating us as though there was anything special about any one of us. The problem with my mother's belief was that, in fact, we were all different; treating us as though we were the same left my sisters and me feeling terribly confused and out of touch with any sense of who we were.

Our thoughts and feelings took low priority, and I learned early not to bother my mother or anyone else with my feelings. When I expressed myself emotionally, she would say, "If you don't stop that nonsense, I'll give you something to cry about." Most people thought I was happy because I was bubbly, smiled a lot and pretended to be okay. In truth, I just kept all my sad and lonely feelings of being misunderstood bottled up inside.

Other people genuinely seemed to like me. They told me I was sweet and kind, and because of my long, black hair and large, expressive, dark brown eyes, they often commented that I was pretty. But I wasn't even allowed to enjoy a compliment. I could always hear my mother's stern voice saying, "Now don't you go and get a big head," which to me, as a child, meant I shouldn't believe what other people told me.

School became my refuge, a safe place where I could escape for a few hours a day. I was a good student, always pleasant, and I loved school. The only things I can remember ever getting in trouble for was chewing gum and talking to other students when I wasn't supposed to. Usually I was the bright-eyed child who was staring at the teacher but whose mind was far away in never-never land. Nevertheless, my teachers seemed to like me, and I hoped that someday one of them would see the real me and tell me who I really was. But again, my prayers went unanswered. They also were too busy being responsible for all the children to have time to consider us as individuals.

Although at five foot one my mother was a petite woman, she seemed bigger than life to me, and the words that came out of her mouth left sharp, lasting impressions. She said I "shouldn't be so friendly," and that I was "overbearing," meaning I should tone down my personality, which was "too much" for her. She didn't appreciate my sensitive and emotional nature either. To her, it was a sign that I was weak and needed to toughen up or, in her words, have a "thicker skin." The only way I knew to interpret her attitude was to believe there was something wrong with me, especially when her comments were said in an unpleasant tone of voice. My spirit was broken and my self-concept was so poor that I couldn't see anything positive about myself. I assumed that my character was flawed at best and doomed at worst, and I spent a lot of time trying to hide parts of myself for fear of being criticized for the way I was.

The subconscious messages I received early in life manifested themselves in my behavior. When I wanted to speak out and say what I believed, I held myself back, because I didn't want to be perceived as overbearing. Besides, I now believed I wasn't supposed to be heard, so, I thought, who would listen anyway? I had difficulty speaking up in classes throughout my school years and later in college. When the teacher called on me to answer a question, I would get a fearful and nervous feeling in my stomach. Even when I knew the answer I was afraid of what might happen if the teacher didn't like what I had to say. Attending a large university like Ohio State made it easy for me to lose myself in the crowd, and I was relieved not to have to worry about being singled out in class by a professor.

The problem surfaced again later when I graduated from college and went to work. In my first job as an elementary school teacher, standing up in front of thirty children was frightening. I can remember feeling my knees trembling and asking myself, "Why am I so afraid of these little people?" Later, when I first became a counselor, I knew I had a problem. One day, while I was leading a group discussion, someone started to talk about her mother and I could not hold back my tears. Feeling embarrassed and totally humiliated, I just wanted to run away and hide. Already fearful of being overly sensitive and emotional, I was living my worst nightmare. All of the negative beliefs about who I was became my own self-fulfilling prophecy. Unconsciously, I was creating conditions in my life to validate what I believed to be true about myself inside.

Hearing negative comments during most of the first eighteen years of my life left me with a tremendous case of low self-esteem, pain and confusion about who I was, well into my late twenties. Because I had learned that it was not okay to be myself, in order to please others I pretended to be someone I was not. I constantly asked myself, "If I'm not who I thought I was, and I can't be who I was told to be, then who am I?" I began a lifelong journey to discover the answer.

Part of my quest included studying to become a counselor. I hoped that by learning how to understand others I might better understand myself.

After more than thirteen years as a counselor, I was looking for a better personality evaluation system to help me in my work. Many students were coming to me seeking direction after they entered college without clear career goals. I used various methods to help them uncover their strengths and weaknesses. Although I used several instruments to access personality, some placed too much emphasis on what was wrong with people, and others were too complicated.

In 1988, I attended a training seminar in Laguna Beach, California. After getting lost and arriving late, I entered the room in time to hear a group of about thirty people finish introducing themselves to each other. All eyes turned to me as I made my way forward from the back of the room. After I introduced myself and told the group what kind of work I did and how I found out about the training, I took my seat. The seminar leader thanked me and then introduced a tall, gray-haired man named Don Lowry, the creator of the True Colors Personality System. As he talked about the history, philosophy and benefits of the program, I began to get excited.

Then we were asked to prioritize the four color-coded personality cards we had received with our course materials. As I studied and sorted the cards, I felt torn between choosing Gold or Blue as my strongest color. Suddenly, I realized that this simple exercise was highlighting the very confusion I had about my self-identity.

The next step was to explain to another person why we had arranged the cards in the order we did. As I tried to explain, I began to understand why at first I had chosen the Gold card. Gold represented the personality I was trying to emulate because of my mother's influence, but the Blue card described who I really was. What a revelation!

The simple True Colors system revealed the source of the pain I had experienced for many years. Like the proverbial light bulb flashing in my brain, I instantly saw that who I truly am — the person I had not allowed myself to be — is different from the personality that my mother had tried to reshape and mold me to be.

The leader then grouped us with others who had the same first color. The exchange I observed and experienced was truly amazing. I immediately connected with the four other women and two men in my Blue group. It was exhilarating to be with others who were so much like me. They shared many of my thoughts and feelings, and we took turns taking the words right out of each other's mouths. These six people, total strangers to me just a few hours earlier, totally understood who I was, and I understood them as well. It was like coming home to a comfortable place where you didn't need to explain who you were because everyone already knew you — the real you.

Each of the four color groups then shared information about themselves with the full group. This enlightening experience became a real eye opener when the Gold group spoke. The Golds sounded very much like my mother, except that they stressed the positive things about who they were. I gained great insight into my mother's personality. I finally understood our differences and how the person she wanted me to be was simply an image of herself.

Like everyone, my mother was not trained to be a parent; and, also like everyone, she did the best she could with the knowledge she had. Like other parents of her generation, she did not understand that children are born with personality traits that are part of their individual nature and cannot be changed. These inner qualities are what make each child unique and special; when understood, these traits provide clues to guide children in the direction they need to take to express their true selves.

I was stunned. Don Lowry presented powerful information in a way I had never before understood. I immediately recognized the benefit in helping individuals reclaim their true selves, which could spare many like me from the lifelong pain, struggle, and wasted time of trying to figure it out for themselves. Because we don't understand the unique qualities of our children, we often try to bend them to match our own personalities. If parents could be taught to recognize, understand and validate their children for who they truly are, imagine the special gifts that could be nurtured and developed.

What a shame to have to wait for a mid-life crisis in order to understand yourself and what you want to do with your life. Imagine learning early in life how to channel all of your positive traits, natural strengths and talents in a meaningful direction. Finding the work you love would not be the difficult, confusing, and overwhelming task that so many people experience.

Discovering my True Colors was a turning point in my life that showed me I am an extroverted, friendly, sensitive and emotional person — and, even more significant, that these are positive traits. No one had ever told me these were my strengths. In fact, what I learned from my mother was the opposite. What she called overbearing I now see as being friendly, extroverted and able to talk to anyone. And rather than indicating weakness, my sensitive and emotional characteristics help me connect with others and their feelings, which is my special gift.

I began to realize how I had abandoned the best parts of myself out of fear. My inability to accept my strengths as strengths went against the grain of who I am and created much of the struggle and most of the low self-esteem issues in my life. It felt as though a burden had been lifted and I could breathe a sigh of relief, relax and be myself. I felt totally validated for the first time in my life.

My low self-esteem made it impossible for me to see what I naturally did well. These talents were hidden from me. Those things I was good at I wrote off as being no big deal and thought anybody could do them. I now know that isn't the truth. True Colors showed me how my natural gifts and talents fit into the world.

This information enhanced my counseling skills and clarified the direction of my work. I used to think that becoming an administrator was an option, but now I know that administration would not utilize my best talents and I can focus on what I do best. I specialize in career counseling and help others figure out who they are and the work they love to do. What a joy to use all my favorite skills by motivating, inspiring and bringing out the best in others! As a counselor, educator, and author, I utilize the same skills. Once we know what our talents are, we can see how easily they transfer into various career options.

I have rewritten the scripts for my life and I have a new self-fulfilling prophecy — one which says, "I am already good enough just the way I am. The beliefs that created my negative self-image were not the truth. Who I am is perfect to do the work I am meant to do. I need only to have faith — the opposite of fear — and trust in my true self."

Understanding who you are is the first and most important step in discovering your ideal career. The chapters in this book are designed to help you recognize your true self, while raising your self-esteem. Self-knowledge and understanding will assist you in finding the work that allows you to express who you are and use your natural strengths and talents. Although this program was the catalyst for my understanding myself and healing major wounds I received early in life, it is not a panacea. Once you know this information, you may still feel blocked by your own fear. I was. Beginning with chapter Ten, I will share the tools that worked to unblock the fear that initially kept me stuck. Follow your own true colors to ultimately create your life's work, which in turn will bring more happiness, passion, and excitement than you can imagine. Success is certain to follow.

2

Your True Colors

‹ ‹ ‹ ‹ ‹ ‹ ‹ ‹ ‹ ‹ ‹ ‹ ‹ › › › › › › › › › › › ›

You have personality traits that make you unique and special, but like most people, you may not know what they are. Why? Because they are hidden. I see these qualities in people every day but it's more important that they see for themselves. It's time to discover for yourself the special traits within you — your personal seeds of opportunity.

Discovering Your True Colors

1. Remove the four *True Colors* cards.
2. Look at the pictures on the front of each card and read the words on the back.
3. Each card describes a part of your personality, but ask yourself which of these cards best portrays you and the things that are important to you. Set aside the card that best captures who you are, not who you wish to be. The values and behaviors represented by your first color will be truer to your real self. Choose the card that best characterizes you.
4. Next, select the card that is least like you.
5. Rank in order the other two cards so that the four color

cards are arranged in order from the one most like you to the one least like you.

6.   Write down the order in which you arranged the cards.

7.   You may want to take the test provided in Appendix B of this book if you are confused about the order of your cards.

FIRST COLOR	SECOND COLOR	THIRD COLOR	FOURTH COLOR

You have now discovered your True Colors profile. The first color represents the characteristics that you relate to most strongly. The first color is also called your "primary" or brightest color. Your self-esteem will derive from the inherent traits of your primary color.

Your second color will influence how you go about expressing your first color. You will see less of yourself in the third and fourth colors. No primary color is better than another. Each personality has different strengths and preferences. I often refer to people by their first two colors because most of their behavior is expressed in those two colors.

The combination of your first two colors will have a big impact on your career decisions. Take the example of me and two of my Blue friends. Although we all have the same primary Blue color, each of us has a different second color. All of us want to help others improve their lives, but we have chosen different career paths to accomplish this goal. My Blue-Orange friend is a professional speaker, consultant and trainer for corporations. She prefers work that is fast-paced and high-energy and includes a lot of variety. Humor and entertainment are also a major part of her presentation.

A Blue-Gold friend of mine is a social worker because she loves taking care of people. Being responsible for the welfare and safety issues of others appeals to her Gold color.

My first two colors are Blue and Green. Career counseling satisfies my Blue while researching and writing this book appeals to my Green.

We must stay true to our natural strengths and never lose sight of what we do best, but we can draw on the skills of the other colors when needed. For example, school requires us to use more of our Green and Gold skills, whereas a romantic relationship calls on our Blue skills, and situations that demand us to be more physical and spontaneous, such as sports, require our Orange skills.

Sitting around a table at a family gathering, we decided to use the True Colors cards to get to know each other better. As we began, I chuckled when I noticed how differently each person handled his or her set of cards.

Sheila looked at the front of the cards, instantly related to the pictures, then quickly decided how she was going to arrange them. When we asked her if she was going to read the back, she said she could but she already knew her order. Sheila is Orange.

Jim, on the other hand, read and analyzed every word on the back of each card, thinking, "This is too simple to be valid." He reluctantly made a decision after pondering each card with a questioning look on his face. Jim is Green.

Diana, using her intuition about the pictures, read the words only to reinforce her initial feelings about each card. Diana is Blue.

As Mark meticulously looked at one card at a time, he studied the pictures and picked out specific details. When finished looking at the front, he turned the card over and examined the back in the same manner before going to the next one. After carefully and methodically looking at all four, he made a decision. Mark is Gold.

These people demonstrate the different characteristics of the four personalities. They thought the cards were just a game because they were having so much fun, but they soon discovered how much they learned about themselves and each other.

Your First Card Represents Your Strengths— What You Do Well.

Your first card is the one you connect with the most for several reasons. Because the pictures and descriptions relate to the things that are most valuable and important to you, you tend to focus your attention on these things more than those on the other cards. Your primary color represents your core personality preferences and the behavior that comes naturally to you.

This primary color card gives you clues about what you should be doing the majority of your time at work.

Your Fourth Card Represents Your Weaknesses— What You Do Not Do Well.

Fourth color characteristics suggest areas where you will encounter many of your challenges and difficulties at work, at home and in relationships. It is imperative that you do not do work that requires you to spend the majority of your time doing the things represented on this card. Some situations will require that you adopt the attitudes and behaviors of this color, but you should never lose sight of your true self — as represented by your primary color.

Extroversion vs. Introversion

Some people are naturally more outgoing than others. Extroverts are stimulated and energized by people and the external environment. Picture someone who likes to talk a lot and comes alive around other people.

Introverts don't like to talk much and prefer to be alone. One way is not better than the other; they are just different preferences for ways of behaving. Some occupations, however, are better suited for introverts than extroverts (and vice versa), even from within the same personality color. Each color includes both introverts and extroverts, and everything in between. Which are you?

Oranges and Blues have a higher percentage of extroverts, and Golds and Greens tend to be more introverted. Extroverts will prefer careers with a lot of people contact, whereas introverts need less.

Your Roles vs. Your Identity

Your identity is who you are. Your identity determines how you will naturally behave in a particular role, but a role does not change your identity. Sometimes you are forced to play several roles in life simultaneously, such as worker, parent and lover. It is important not to confuse the roles you play with your identity.

The role of worker is one that confuses many people about their identity, because many people are in work positions that go against the grain of who they are. For example, Joe thought his primary color was Gold because he is a sales manager. While it's true that he performs job duties suitable for a Gold personality, his job as a manager is only a role he plays and not who he is. When I helped him to see that he is a free-spirited Orange personality who will naturally feel restricted in a management job, Joe was finally able to understand why he was not able to express his true self at work. He made a decision to return to the sales position that he had enjoyed before he was promoted to manager.

Finding work that fits your identity (instead of trying to squeeze your identity into your job) will allow you to express your true self, will lessen the discomfort and dissatisfaction you might otherwise feel, and will naturally result in positive self-esteem.

This book emphasizes self-esteem because I feel it is important to recognize what is good and positive about yourself. Most of us already know what is wrong with us all too well. When you are in-esteem you live a positive and productive life that expresses your true self. When you are out-of-esteem, you live in fear and self-doubt, and you don't live up to your potential.

The best way I know to raise your self-esteem is to do what you love. That's why finding your life's work is so critical. It is difficult, if not impossible, to do something that you hate all day and still have high self-esteem.

3

Your Hidden Talents

‹ ‹ ‹ ‹ ‹ ‹ ‹ ‹ ‹ ‹ ‹ ‹ › › › › › › › › › › › › ›

God has already revealed His will to us
concerning our vocation and Mission, by causing it to
be "written in our members." We are to begin deci-
phering our unique Mission by studying our talents
and skills, and particularly which ones (or One) we
most rejoice to use.

Richard N. Bolles
What Color Is Your Parachute?

I've seen many people who hate their jobs but are afraid to leave because they don't know what else to do. Finding your ideal work should be the result of discovering your own hidden talents, never something you stumble upon by accident or luck. You've heard that to be successful in your work, you should do what you love. Not a novel idea. Twenty-five hundred years ago, Confucius said, "Choose a job you love to do and you will never work another day in your life," yet this age-old wisdom has not become widely practiced. Many people still don't know what they love to do.

Robert came to me confused. He was painfully bored with the third accounting job he'd had in the past four years. Although he began each job with good intentions, he lost interest after the novelty wore off, typically after three or four months on the job. He was convinced that he needed a complete change of direction. During our first session, I noticed that he had a tremendous amount of energy, the gift of gab and a good sense of humor.

I explained how I was going to use the True Colors Personality System to help me understand his natural strengths, what he enjoyed and what was important to him.

I asked him to prioritize the cards. After briefly looking at all four cards, he grabbed the Orange one and put it last, explaining, "This is the kind of person I used to be, but that behavior got me into too much trouble. Now I'm more like what it says on the Gold card."

"Robert," I said, "I understand that you may want to develop your character by adopting more Gold card characteristics, but we must start with where you are before we can talk about where you want to go. First you must be clear about who you are. I'd like to begin by hearing your story."

"I was the bad apple in the family," Robert began. "You know, the one who caused all the problems. Both of my parents were strict. My father was a perfectionist, former military man, who had high standards and expectations for his children. My mother was a traditional homemaker who stayed home and raised me, my brother and sister. Maybe because I was the oldest my dad seemed to be hardest on me. Nothing I did was ever good enough. If I got a B in a class he would say, 'Why didn't you get an A?' Even if I got the highest grade in the class he would say, 'Why can't you do that all the time?'

"I felt as though I grew up literally looking at the world from behind the fence that surrounded our suburban yard in southern California. My sister, brother and I were never allowed to leave our yard and play with other kids or have them come over to our house. When I went to school it was like escaping from prison. I was totally afraid of my father and the only place I could ever play and have fun was at school, except I also got into a lot of trouble. I was always big for my age, and I was known as the class clown who was either telling jokes, throwing spit balls, pulling some girl's hair, or dancing on the table when the teacher left the room. I also had my fair share of fights on the playground. It seemed like I spent as much time in the principal's office as I did in class.

"I felt out of control at school, even though I knew my dad would punish me. He would say I was a loser and a flake who would never amount to anything in life. By the time I was in tenth grade, I had been expelled from school twice. The last time I was dismissed, I transferred to a high school that dealt with 'kids like me' who had discipline problems. The new school turned out to be the best thing that could have happened to me.

"I had a really cool math teacher, who took an interest in me. He was the only one I ever thought believed in me and I did well in his math class because he made it so much fun. Because of his encouragement I went to college and got a business degree in accounting. Here I am, twenty-nine years old, and at least I have a degree, but I can just hear my father say, 'See, I told you you're a loser; you can't even keep a job.'"

I explained to Robert that his acting-out behavior while growing up was a result of his low self-esteem rather than an expression of his true self. "You already know enough negative things about yourself," I said. "Now let's talk about your positive attributes."

Robert initially felt uncomfortable about tooting his own horn, but then he said, "I guess I'm good at persuading and convincing people to do things. I also like to cheer people up and make them laugh. Sometimes I'm accused of saying things inappropriately, like making a funny comment in the middle of a serious and boring business meeting. And unlike some people, who can only do one thing at a time, I like to have several things going on at the same time — maybe this is not such a good thing. I guess I get bored easily and I'm happiest when I'm busy."

I assured Robert that each quality he had identified in himself was great, and if he were able to express his true personality more in his work, he would ultimately feel better about himself. I said, "I can see that you are an outgoing, adventurous and free-spirited person. These traits are typical of your Orange personality and yet you've been tied to a desk and dealing with detail information all day. Your work requires you to use your weakest and least rewarding skills, those more natural for the Gold personality. You obviously have been suppressing your true nature in your accounting job."

Robert agreed and said, "Maybe that's why I get so many headaches at work."

Robert considered several career options that better suited him and used the career center to research those that interested him most. We agreed that marketing sounded like the best match for his talents and an area he could easily move into with his business background. On my advice, he interviewed a successful marketing specialist and discovered that he could use his creativity and good sense of humor to produce advertising to sell products and services. He found it especially appealing to interact with lots of people on a variety of projects, using print, audio, video, and broadcast media to advertise for clients. Feeling very encouraged, he was excited about pursuing this new career path.

The last time I heard from Robert, he called to tell me how happy he was that he had landed a position with an advertising agency. He explained, "I actually look forward to going to work every day now. I used to think there was something wrong with me because I couldn't sit and concentrate for long periods of time in my accounting job. Now I can see it was the wrong job for me." He thanked me for rescuing him from dying a slow death, and I congratulated him for being willing to get in touch with his true self and find work that allows him to express who he really is.

When you discover the truth about who you are, it will change your life.

‹ ‹ ‹ › › ›

When I spoke to Michelle, a slender thirty-year-old woman, it became obvious that her true talents were hidden from her. She had been groomed ever since she was a child to take over the family business. She was the third generation to operate the lucrative restaurant that her family had owned for more than forty years. Her grandfather was the founder, and her father had managed the business until five years ago when his health began to fail and Michelle had to take over.

"Both my father and grandfather loved running the business and dedicated their whole lives to making it prosperous," she explained. "I know my life would be set if I could do what they did. Unfortunately, it's not working for me because I'm miserable and extremely cranky all day at work."

"Is there anything you do like about your work?" I asked.

"At first it was okay, because it was new and challenging," she replied. "But I'm the kind of person who is interested in so many things that I can't decide what I really want to do. Even as a child I had a curious mind and I was good at everything in school. I did as well in English and history as I did in science and math. Yes, I was the nerdy, introverted kid with glasses who got straight A's. I've always been an avid reader; when my mother wanted to punish me she would take my books away. She knew that toys didn't matter, but without my books I was lost."

"I understand you were good in everything you studied, but did you have a favorite subject in school?" I asked.

"Yes," she said. "Science fascinated me and I used to dream of one day discovering a cure for some disease. I suppose that's why I majored in biology in college. My parents didn't care what I got my degree in because they expected me eventually to take over the business. They just wanted me to have an education."

I asked Michelle what she disliked about managing the restaurant. "The things I hate most are those I do routinely on a daily basis. This is a hands-on business, where the owner has to stay involved or it doesn't work. I really hate making shift schedules. Invariably someone wants to come in late, leave early or take the day off, which requires me to juggle other people around to maintain adequate coverage. Supervising people is another thing I detest. Some people don't seem to want to work, and to others I have to explain the same thing over and over again before they understand it. I'm not the most patient person and maybe I expect too much from people. My job is not hard work. After all, it's not rocket science, you know. It is fast-paced and a lot of busy work. I am continually putting out fires all day. If it's not equipment problems, it's a disgruntled employee or an unhappy customer. I feel like I'm going brain dead and wasting my time doing this work."

It was clear to me that Michelle's family had good intentions in having her take over the business, but because they did not account for her real talents, they were pushing her to follow the wrong path.

Michelle wanted to figure out what was missing in her work. She chose the Green card as the one that described her best. Once she understood her personality traits, Michelle was ready to answer two key questions that would lead her to her ideal career: "What motivates you?" and "What do you enjoy doing?"

What Motivates You?

To know what we need for our work to be satisfying, we must understand who we are. A major reason we don't understand ourselves and others better is that we are unaware of natural personality differences between individuals. It is a mistake to assume that we all want and need the same things. What motivates one person may not move another person at all. True Colors explains how the four distinct personalities have different motivators that drive their behavior. Each personality (color) also has preferred ways of doing things by using unique gifts and talents. Together these traits provide valuable clues about the kind of careers that would be rewarding for each color.

It is easier to understand ourselves if we know what motivates how we think, feel and behave. Everyone has personality traits that I refer to as "hidden motivators," because they are not visible yet they explain why we do what we do. Sometimes others notice these traits in us long before we do. These motivators are our true values, which remain consistent regardless of the situations we're in or the roles we play. We take our true values with us wherever we go and whatever we do. We reveal our values through what we care about, what is important to us, what we pay attention to, and how we spend our time.

When the values that motivate us are not met, we begin to feel dissatisfied with our lives and our work. We begin to say things like "My job is not challenging," "There is no meaning or purpose in what I do every day," "My work is too routine and boring," "I'm wasting my time in a job that has no future," or "What else can I do?" All these statements allude to a sense of being off track or not on purpose in our work.

I asked Michelle to identify the true values that strongly motivate her behavior. She explained, "I've had an extremely curious mind all my life and I have to be mentally challenged or I get bored. Once I've learned something, I need to find a new challenge to keep life interesting."

Michelle listed the following values that motivate her: knowledge, intelligence, abstract ideas, independence, vision, imagination, curiosity and mental challenge.

Understanding our motivators is only part of the process. We must also explore the things we enjoy doing.

What Do You Enjoy Doing?

This clue is somewhat easier to recognize because it is more obvious in our behavior. We all have a natural propensity toward certain things that we do well. These are the natural gifts and talents that make us unique and special. They are our inherent how-to-do tools built into our personalities to express who we are. Our talents are the skills we enjoy using and our preferred manners of doing things. It is easy to underestimate them because we do these things so easily and effortlessly. This sometimes leads us to believe there is nothing special about our own particular strengths. Certain activities are enjoyable to us precisely because they utilize our natural gifts and talents. They fit, so they're fun.

Those who do what they naturally do well often say they feel more like they're getting paid to have fun rather than working. But even having fun has a different meaning to each type. What is fun for one personality can feel like hard work to another. A person who is naturally funny sees the humor in the mundane things of everyday life. Of course, it would be easy to imagine this person as a comedian. Yet someone who only sees the serious side of life would find it difficult, if not impossible, to be a good comedian. This is why imitation can be so dangerous. It is a struggle to try to be someone you're not. Imitation, rather than being the sincerest form of flattery, is more likely a sign that we don't naturally fit. If we are trying to imitate someone, it usually means we're going against our true selves. When we stay in line with our true selves, we no longer need to copy anyone else.

We often think we are capable of doing a particular kind of work just because someone else can do it. It is difficult to see ourselves objectively and assess our own strengths and weaknesses. By focusing on our positive attributes (what is right about us rather than what is wrong), the True Colors Personality System serves as an effective tool to reveal why we are naturally good at some things and not others. Just because a job is available doesn't mean it will be satisfying to us.

When I asked Michelle her favorite skills, she said, "Oh, that's easy. I love to analyze everything. I am constantly picking ideas apart either with other people or in my own mind. I also love the challenge of problem solving." She listed the following skills she enjoys: learning, intellectualizing, diagnosing, interpreting ideas, researching, analyzing and problem solving.

Notice that these skills are not used only in one occupation. They are called transferable skills because they can be used in several different careers. Your natural talent provides the flexibility to utilize what you do best in many areas. Many people get jobs and then try to bend the jobs to fit their true selves. A better strategy is to understand yourself and then find work that fits. Because most people will have several careers rather than staying in one job until they retire, this kind of adaptability is extremely important today.

What Is a Life's Work?

We refer to what we do to make a living by different terms. The most commonly used word is "job." There is a negative connotation associated with the word "job," because statistics show that most people are dissatisfied with their jobs. In fact, Monday morning has come to symbolize a return to something undesirable. Dr. Deepak Chopra says that more people have heart attacks on Monday morning at nine o'clock than any other time of the week. What are most people doing Monday morning at nine o'clock? Returning to their jobs, of course. Chopra says that a survey revealed that all these people had one thing in common — they hated their jobs. I prefer to avoid the word "job."

I think of jobs as something we do to pay the bills until we find careers. In the words of mythologist Joseph Campbell, "The person who takes a job in order to live — that is to say, for the money — has turned himself into a slave." I know many from the baby boomer generation who are struggling with this issue. We need and long for something more.

Career-minded people are usually more conscious of the need for some personal fulfillment from their work. Most career occupations require training or a college education; time and money are involved in career preparation, which suggests a higher level of deliberation, commitment and longevity. Still, one may have several careers in a lifetime.

I prefer the term "life's work" over "job" and "career." A life's work is the ultimate career, a conscious effort to unite the spiritual part of who you are, your being, with your practical need to make a living. In other words, a life's work draws on your awareness of your inner strengths as a guide to your unique expression of your authentic self.

Many people live their lives as though who they are and what they do for a living are separate entities. Because they don't feel connected with the work they perform all day, their occupations ultimately have no meaning. Instead, they go through the motions of performing habitual tasks day in and day out while wishing for something more, something better, something that isn't such a drain. I sometimes refer to these people as "the walking dead" because of the lack of life coming out of them. Some will say they put their lives on hold until they leave work. I can't imagine a more miserable person than one who spends the majority of the work day unhappy. "Unhappy" easily correlates to "ineffective," not for lack of effort or ability, but for lack of fit. Nobody wins in a misfit situation. The worker is not happy, the boss doesn't have a productive employee, and the end user or customer ultimately is cheated.

Meaningful work allows for meaningful contributions, leading to meaningful results. The key is to find work that is meaningful for you, based on the natural characteristics of your true self.

You can think of your life's work as more of a calling, a path or a mission, as Richard Bolles says in *What Color Is Your Parachute?* Your life's work is a way to express who you are mentally, emotionally and spiritually, through your unique strengths and talents, to make a contribution to society. It creates a sense of connection with your work, being purposeful with your life, and sharing your best self with the world. In a deeper sense, discovering your calling allows you to express your true nature.

Michelle found several careers that intrigued her. Her interest in science drew her to consider the roles of physician's assistant, medical doctor, veterinarian and physical therapist; in the end, she chose to make her life's work as a biomedical researcher.

"As a biomedical researcher," she explained, "I will be looking for ways to treat or, better yet, cure and prevent human diseases. This career suits me perfectly, satisfies all of my core values and allows me to use my best skills. I've always loved learning and acquiring knowledge; becoming a researcher will pay me to do what I do best. Maybe someday I will live out my childhood fantasy and become famous for finding a cure for a disease like cancer or AIDS."

With her bachelor's degree in biology, Michelle was able to enroll in graduate school to eventually earn a Ph.D. in the same field.

All of us are here to discover who we truly are and to use our special gifts to make a contribution to the world. Your life's work encompasses your overall life, not just the work you do. It is the integration of your lifestyle and your work.

Once you discover your life's work, you likely will do it — in some form — for the rest of your life. As you age, you may not continue on a full-time basis, but neither will you rush to retire from something you feel passionate about. Many people who are wealthy yet continue to work when there is no need for more money do so because their life's work rewards them in other important ways.

Your life's work may not be what you do to make a living; nevertheless, when you are involved in your life's work, you will have a sense of doing something significant with your life. And if you find work that is important to you, chances are you can find a way to get paid for it.

Once you learn the clues to what motivates you and what your natural gifts and talents are, you too will be on a path to finding your life's work.

How Can I Use My Uniqueness to Be Successful in My Work?

Expressing your uniqueness is what makes you successful. There is no one else who can do exactly what you can do, because no other person has your life experiences mixed with your unique strengths. Consciously developing and using your own natural gifts and talents can make you stand out and be successful in your work.

Oprah Winfrey is a good example of this. A lot of people host talk shows, but Oprah showcases her natural skills and expresses herself in a style uniquely her own. She once said that doing a talk show was "like breathing" to her. This is what it feels like to do your life's work. Doesn't Oprah make it look like fun? Her phenomenally high ratings and incredible financial success result from her expressing her own uniqueness. Please be encouraged. You too can express your own unique combination of talent and experience, and reap rewards that will be meaningful and satisfying to you.

How Can I Work Smarter — Not Harder?

The people I see who are most dissatisfied with their jobs usually are working much too hard, because their job duties require them to use their weaknesses rather than their strengths, which is hard work! Whenever we do not express our true selves we experience anxiety, leading to stress. Forcing ourselves to express values that go against the grain of who we are and using skills that don't come naturally are the biggest contributors to on-the-job stress.

Stressed out by her job, Margaret came to see me. Although she was an excellent third grade teacher who had earned much recognition from her peers and superiors for her skills and dedication to her profession, she said, "It's not enjoyable for me anymore. I never thought I would see the day when I would dread going to work."

"But you told me you loved children and teaching," I said. "What has changed to cause you to hate your work?"

"After teaching for almost fifteen years I felt a change might be good for me. Several years ago, I earned an advanced degree in education. When the principal of my school was promoted to a position with the Board of Education, I was offered her job. It paid more money and, at first, I looked forward to the change. It's only been a year but I'm already burned out."

I asked her what bothered her about her job as principal.

"Confrontation is very difficult for me," she said. "It's not an issue with children, but have you ever tried telling an adult what to do? It's those who don't do their jobs that cause all the problems. I don't like conflict and it's stressful for me to have to confront these people. Some have yelled and screamed at me because on their job evaluations I reported their unprofessional behavior. I also dislike all the bureaucracy involved with this position. The extra money is not worth it to me."

"If you enjoy teaching children, why don't you go back to that?" I asked.

"Well, it's kind of embarrassing, but several friends and family members have a lot of confidence in me and they tell me I can do this job. I feel that I would be letting them down if I gave up," she replied.

After we discussed her characteristics as a Blue personality, she confirmed that what she really enjoys is encouraging and supporting growth in others. Dealing with conflict and confrontation is too stressful for her sensitive nature. She needs peace and harmony in her work. It also became clear that teaching utilizes her natural abilities, whereas administration does not. She admitted that she has a tendency to be a people pleaser and she allows others to influence her too much. "I guess I need to start listening to my own intuition," she concluded. She made the decision to return to the classroom and resumed her enjoyable life's work teaching children.

Margaret is the epitome of someone who was working much too hard because the skills required of a principal were her weakest areas of competence, and the least enjoyable to her. Her strengths were more consistent with the skills needed to be a teacher.

When she returned to the classroom, Margaret was able to maximize her strengths and minimize her weaknesses by doing what she does best.

As we continue, you will learn your strengths and weaknesses so that you can make smarter decisions about your own life's work. Then when you choose to work harder, it can be to achieve superior results rather than simply to overcome your weaknesses.

〈 〈 〈 〉 〉 〉

Dave was a flight attendant for an international airline. During the six years he had flown, he had visited many interesting places and made good money, but he was experiencing a lot of stress in his work.

"I feel a little guilty complaining about my job, because so many of my friends envy me," he said. "All the traveling looks glamorous to them, but I'm frustrated and stressed out. I can't figure out what's wrong with me. After all, my job has been stable and I have good benefits. What more can I ask for?"

When we uncovered his true colors, Dave learned the source of his stress. "What is important to me," he said, "is to have a familiar place to go every day, with a predictable schedule. Flying requires me to go to different states and sometimes different countries. I dislike unfamiliar hotels. I like sleeping in my own bed and having control over the kind of food I eat. There is too much unpredictability and lack of routine in this work."

I explained to Dave that nothing is wrong with him. The important elements and stress-producers for him are typical of the Gold personality. Some people don't like predictability and routine work, but Dave truly values these things. One person's joy is another's stress.

Dave didn't have to look far to find his ideal career. He became a manager with the same airline. "Now I have everything I need — a good salary, stability in my work, good benefits, the same daily schedule, and no requirement to travel."

Can I still do my life's work after I retire?

It is never too late to do your life's work. Not many retired people sit in a rocking chair from the time they retire until they die. Studies show that those who continue to engage themselves in meaningful activities after retirement live longer. Although many people have strong security needs and find it risky to give up familiar work, retirement is the perfect opportunity for some to do what they love.

Frank spent his professional life as a manager for a large corporation. Although he was not totally dissatisfied with his job, how he spent his time away from work was the real clue to what he loved to do. His need for security motivated him to become an expert at investing his own retirement money in stocks, bonds and mutual funds. His friends knew how successful he became, because he spent most of his social time talking about investments. They began to ask Frank for advice and consequently made more money than they had with paid professionals. At first, Frank was not willing to give up his job security and retirement benefits. But now that he has retired from his job, he gets paid to give people financial advice and is much happier doing what he has always loved.

4

Self-Esteem Comes in Four Colors

‹ ‹ ‹ ‹ ‹ ‹ ‹ ‹ ‹ ‹ ‹ ‹ ‹ › › › › › › › › › › › ›

Work is integral to the whole tapestry of our lives.
If we have no happiness or joy within ourselves how
can there be any at work? As we enhance our self-
esteem, so we enhance our working lives.

Marsha Sinetar
Do What You Love, and the Money Will Follow

People who love their work say they feel good about who they are and passionate about what they're doing. They often lose track of time when involved with their work. Expressing your true self in your work will raise your self-esteem and lead you to success. On the other hand, if your occupation values and rewards characteristics that you do not naturally possess, your work experience could feel like a long, hard swim upstream.

What promotes self-esteem in one color does not similarly affect another. In other words, what makes me feel good about myself won't necessarily make you feel good about yourself. Which of the following examples is most like you?

Orange: "Today I made best salesperson of the week by selling more in three hours than I did the whole day yesterday!"

Blue: "Helping someone who really needed it meant I had to go against company policy, but the person was more important to me than some outdated rule."

Gold: "I'm proud to say I was able to increase efficiency by fifteen percent without increasing the budget."

Green: "While surfing the Web today, I discovered a better way to integrate Information Systems with Production."

Self-esteem comes in different colors, but before we can make sense of this concept it is important to understand what self-esteem is and why it is important.

The California Task Force to Promote Self-Esteem and Personal and Social Responsibility defines self-esteem as "appreciating my own worth and importance and having the character to be accountable for myself and act responsibly towards others."

A simple definition of self-esteem is "having a positive feeling about yourself," which is not something to take lightly. Nathaniel Branden says in *The Psychology of Self Esteem* that self-esteem "directly impacts the most important relationship you will ever have — your relationship with yourself. There is no value judgment more important to man than the estimate he passes on himself." The more you like yourself the higher your self-esteem will be.

Liking ourselves begins with the knowledge of who we are and what is important to us. When our values are in conflict with others' values, their values will never feel quite as important to us. Betraying our own values or selling out to please others causes internal conflict, which lowers our self-esteem. In career decision-making, if we choose our work to please anyone besides ourselves, it leads to dissatisfaction and low self-esteem.

An attractive, well-dressed young woman walked into my office one day and immediately burst into tears. I was flabbergasted because she appeared to be confident and successful, with high self-esteem.

When Barbara regained her composure, I asked why she was upset. She apologized profusely, then said, "Thank you for letting me cry. I guess I needed to do that. I can't talk to anyone in my family about this problem and I don't dare break down at work or they'll think I'm crazy."

I asked Barbara why anyone would think she was crazy for crying.

"You don't know the kind of people I work with," she said. "I'm an engineer and I work with other engineers. These people don't express their emotions and I know they wouldn't understand my feelings. I work for a local aerospace company and I don't feel like I fit in."

"What is it about your job that makes you feel like a misfit?" I asked.

"I don't have anything in common with the guys I work with. They really like their work and I hate it. My job involves designing and developing commercial and military aircraft. It is highly technical and analytical work, which I don't enjoy."

I asked Barbara why she became an engineer.

"My parents encouraged me to become an engineer because 'engineers run in our family.' I worked hard to get through school to prove to them that I was smart enough to become an engineer, but I can't do this anymore. I don't have any self-confidence left and I feel like I lose my self-esteem every time I go to work."

Barbara's story is common among those who are dissatisfied with their work. We discussed Barbara's true values — the things that were really important to her, which included friendship, interpersonal communication, understanding herself and others, being compassionate and expressing emotions. "These values describe the real me," said Barbara. "When I'm at work, I behave like someone I don't even know."

Much of Barbara's frustration came from not having an outlet to express her true values in her current work as an engineer. Becoming conscious of her own inner nature helped her to understand why her work caused her to have such low self-esteem. For many who are dissatisfied with their work, the problem is not that anything is necessarily wrong with the job itself, the work environment or their working relationships; the "problem" is often that the person is "playing out of position," doing work that doesn't fit who that person truly is. It is common in such circumstances for a person to conclude that "there must be something wrong with me," which results in low self-esteem.

When Barbara learned the true values that gave her self-esteem, it was easier for her to determine the kind of work that would allow her to self-actualize. She said, "I have always loved more than anything to help other people solve their personal problems. In fact, my family and friends come to me for advice. It makes me feel good to be able to help them."

After Barbara quit her engineering job and studied to become a marriage and family therapist, she said, "This work has caused my self-esteem to soar. When I help other people improve their lives it adds meaning and purpose to my own life. Also, I'm glad I made the decision to leave the aerospace industry when I did, because with the cuts in the defense budget I'm sure I would have been laid off like a lot of my friends. This career transition was meant to be."

According to Maslow's hierarchy of needs, self-esteem is our second-highest need, which we pursue after we have satisfied our external, lower needs such as food, shelter and clothing. Because the higher needs are internal, and therefore invisible, we may not be aware of them. Nevertheless, these needs are at the core of our personality and the drive to satisfy these needs motivates our behavior — how we think, feel and act.

Although self-esteem is one of the highest common human needs, each of the four personalities achieves self-esteem in different ways. The four colors don't value everything equally. People of each type will feel more passionately about, and gain more positive self-esteem from, those things that most closely represent their strongest internal values.

The following descriptions show how each color group strives for self-esteem in a positive way.

Maslow's Need Hierarchy

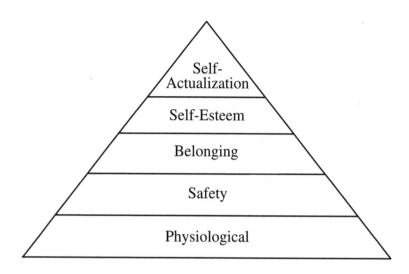

Green: The Need to Be Ingenious

Greens achieve positive self-esteem when they are competent. They want to understand and control the realities of life. Control represents the power to acquire the multiple abilities on which they pride themselves.

Greens feel best about themselves when they are solving problems and when their ideas are recognized. They are complex individualists with great analytical ability.

These abstract thinkers are symbolized by the vision of the genius, the challenge of science, the complexity of models and systems, and the perfection of symmetry, such as is demonstrated in the great pyramids.

Greens thrive on mental competence, as well as on the skills and abilities of others. They are motivated by a quest for knowledge and the abilities to seek it and provide it. The control of knowledge is as important as its acquisition, because such control can be perceived as power.

Blue: The Need to Be Authentic

Blues experience positive self-esteem when they feel authentic. They must find their real selves and live their lives as an expression of their unique identity. For Blues, integrity means unity of inner self and outer expression.

Life is a dream in which they must find meaning. They are sensitive to subtlety and they create roles with special flair in life's drama. Blues enjoy close relationships with those they love and experience a spiritual pride in their nature. Making a difference in the world comes easily to them as they cultivate the potential in themselves and in others.

Blues are natural harmonizers, as symbolized by the vision of peace, the romance of love ballads, the drama of stage and screen, the importance of people and the warmth of a hug and a handshake.

Orange: The Need to Be Skillful

Oranges feel positive self-esteem when, above all, they are free to act on a moment's notice. Action carries its own reward.

Oranges do things for the joy of doing. They choose to be impulsive and to act upon the idea of the moment. They take pride in being highly skilled in a variety of fields. Oranges are master negotiators and adventure is their middle name. They have a zest for life and a desire to test the limits. Their hands-on approach to problem solving and their direct line of reasoning creates excitement and immediate results.

The zest for action and freedom of this free spirit is symbolized by the flight of the eagle, the sensation of hang-gliding, the action and risk of driving a motorcycle, the skillfulness of handling a tool and the freedom of the outdoors.

Gold: The Need to Be Responsible

Golds enjoy positive self-esteem when they feel responsible and when they belong to a social unit. Regardless of which social unit is involved, they must earn their place of belonging by being useful, by fulfilling responsibilities, by being of service, and by caring for others.

Golds value order and they cherish the traditions of home and family. Steadfastness and loyalty are their trademarks. They are parental, demonstrating that they care by ensuring that everyone does the right thing.

These backbones of society are symbolized in the patriotism of the American flag, the structure of groups and organizations, the security of banks and savings books, the responsibility of parenting, the caring of nursing and healing, and the pride of lineage and aristocracy.

As the Gold personality begins to develop, a sense of obligation and duty emerges. Rules by which people interact are of utmost concern to the Gold personality. Security of the family unit and all it stands for is the foundation by which all other interactions are expressed, whether in school, the workplace, the church, social units or society itself.

‹ ‹ ‹ › › ›

I used to be guilty of thinking that everyone acquired self-esteem in the same way, but now I understand that an individual's value preferences determine the outcomes that each is seeking. For example, because I am a primary Blue, I respond to a personal growth seminar because I feel it will improve my life and make me feel good. Personal growth seminars do not appeal to my Green husband, because he says they are "too touchy-feely," but if I tell him about a new idea that will improve his business, I stand a better chance of getting his attention.

These differences have nothing to do with gender. Green women will respond in a way similar to my husband's.

A personal growth seminar would not appeal to a Gold or an Orange unless they knew in advance they were going to obtain some practical skills to use. For example, if you told them how this seminar was going to help them earn more money, that would be a practical reason for them to attend.

Our Ultimate Goal — Self-Actualization

According to Maslow, self-actualization is man's ultimate goal — our highest need. We all want to express our true selves and reach our potential. The key to accomplishing self-actualization lies in how each color achieves self-esteem. A strong, vibrant self-esteem sets a personality on the way to self-actualizing. The actualized self, the self that is yearning to be acknowledged, has been inside us all along but may have been covered up by the confusion of life experiences. Self-actualization is not an unrealistic pipe dream or a static arrival destination. Self-actualization is a state of being, not blocked or full of fear, where life is lived naturally, happily and freely as we achieve our goals and reach our potential.

Each color seeks to self-actualize differently. Self-actualization is the ultimate way of expressing one's self. Pursuing our life's work is a means to actualizing our potential.

In order to discover and appreciate the kind of work that would be satisfying to you, you first must understand how your personality (color) achieves self-esteem and self-actualization, as shown in the following diagram.

The Four Paths to Self-Actualization

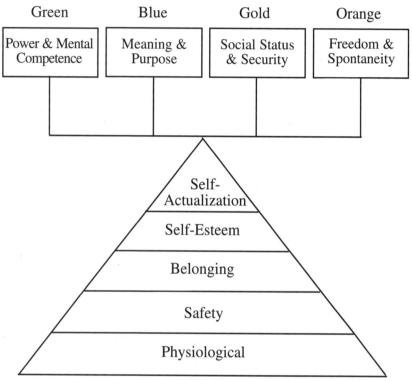

Adapted from *Introduction to Temperament*

Self-esteem comes when you pursue your dreams and passions. Studies show that people who enjoy their work usually feel good about who they are. The opposite is also true. When people engage in work that is not satisfying, it can create a lot of anxiety, which leads to stress and lowers self-esteem.

Self-esteem can also be affected negatively when people are exposed to factors that cause stress. As you by now would expect, each of the four personality types has its own set of stress-inducing elements.

Things That Cause Stress to Greens:

Too many rules
People who get in the way of executing strategy
Incompetence in self or others
Control
Disorganization of system
Rigidity
People who don't value knowledge and learning
Lack of freedom
Not knowing
Off-task distraction
Unfairness
Committee meetings that have no point
Unreasonable emotional outbursts
Labels
No new horizons
Policy and procedures
Welfare mindset
Schedules that make no sense
Stupid people

Things That Cause Stress to Blues:

Disharmony
Judgmental people
Lack of communication
Chaos
Injustice
Rigidity
Isolation
Overly aggressive people
Paperwork and too many details
Cruelty to children and animals
Being yelled at
Being lied to

Conflict
Tunnel vision
Procedures/red tape
Politics
Bossy/negative people
Arrogance
Lack of support
Narrow-mindedness
Lack of understanding
No hugs
Heartlessness
Lack of integrity
Insensitivity
Not being able to express oneself
Lack of romance
Cynics
People who won't grow
Dealing with untrustworthy people
Unresolved confrontations

Things That Cause Stress to Golds:

Inefficiency
Lack of order
Flaky people
Unreliable people
People who are late
Lack of leadership
Non-cooperation
Not knowing what is expected
Slobs
Procrastinators
Waiting
Loud people
Disorganized people

Being told what to do by others
Change
Inconsistency
Things not working out like they think they should
Can't get things done "right"
Not belonging
Lack of control

Things That Cause Stress to Oranges:

Boredom
Being on time
Unnecessary routine
Deadlines
Lack of humor
Slow people
Lack of money
Car problems
Paperwork
Bureaucracy
Lack of sex
Criticism
Negativity
Nagging
Inflexibility
Unbendable rules
Schedules
Waiting
Sameness
Predictability
Traffic

‹ ‹ ‹ › › ›

I know a man who was groomed to be a priest. He said he never thought about being anything else because his family sent him to Catholic school with the expectation that he would someday become a priest. He went to seminary but he always felt like a misfit because he was so different from those who were serious about the profession. He is an easygoing, spontaneous person, and all the rules and structure required by the Church were difficult for him. It got to the point where he was so depressed and stressed out that he developed a drinking problem and had to leave the seminary. When he discovered his true colors (did you guess that his first color is Orange?) he decided he needed more fun and excitement in his work and less structure. He is now enjoying his work as an actor and stuntman for the movies. Today, he is a much happier person who says that if he had understood himself better before going to the seminary, he would have known it went against the grain of who he is.

‹ ‹ ‹ › › ›

Janet became a nurse because she wanted to help people. As she was growing up, she often heard comments about how good she was at helping others with their problems and at doing whatever was necessary to make them feel better. It seemed that she would make a good nurse.

After working three years as a nurse, however, she realized that although she was helping people, something was missing. She was good with the patients, but she felt stressed by the demands made on her at work. True Colors helped her discover that, as a Blue, she was better suited to help people with their emotional needs. Her job, however, required her to take care of her patients' physical needs, such as by giving medication or taking blood pressure and temperature. She was happy to discover that she could stay in the health care field, finding her niche and life's work as a medical social worker. Now, she is paid to use the skills she enjoys most to help people with their emotional problems.

Janet discovered there are many ways to help people, but how she helped people was equally important. When looking for your life's work, it is important to look beyond the job title and consider the specific skills used in an occupation.

What Does It Mean To Be Out-Of-Esteem?

The human being is the only species that can choose to sabotage and betray its own survival. In our ongoing pursuit of self-esteem, sometimes what we choose to make us feel good about ourselves can be destructive. Destructive behaviors can range from the obvious — drug or alcohol abuse — to something as subtle as keeping a job that doesn't utilize one's potential for monetary reasons.

When people suppress their true values, they develop low self-esteem or what I call "being out-of-esteem." When we don't know how to feel good about ourselves in a positive way, we will do it any way we can. Often what surfaces is what Jung refers to as our dark or shadow side. Gaps develop between who people think they should be and who they are. They become fearful and confused about their goals in life, abandon their creativity and lose their feelings of being alive — the sense of what is important to them. The Self-Esteem Task Force concluded that "self-esteem is central to most of the personal and social problems that plague human life in today's world." Many of society's maladies are caused by people who are out-of-esteem, and these are the price society pays for not promoting self-esteem in all people.

How to Read the Following Chapters

Self-understanding is a major step in your journey. The next four chapters are designed to increase your knowledge of who you are. Either read the chapters in the order presented or read them in the order of your card sort. If you have put your cards in the correct order for you, your primary color should prove to be the character you most closely relate to throughout the remainder of the book. Together these chapters will describe more of your personality profile.

You may want to know the personalities of your significant others (children, mate, parents, siblings, friends, co-workers or boss). If so, hand them the True Colors cards. After they sort their colors, read the appropriate chapters to understand their personalities better. Simply by helping you to understand each other better, this information is extremely helpful in resolving conflicts in relationships.

5

The Blue Personality —
To Love and Be Loved

‹ ‹ ‹ ‹ ‹ ‹ ‹ ‹ ‹ ‹ ‹ ‹ › › › › › › › › › › › ›

Of all the people in the world, Blues are the most loving, nurturing and supportive. They do not have to work at it, it is simply their amazing nature — who they are. Everyone has special gifts and talents, and Blues possess extraordinary people skills. They have a tremendous amount of what the author of *Emotional Intelligence*, Dr. Daniel Goleman, calls EQ, or "the ability to read another's innermost feelings and handle relationships smoothly."

Others easily recognize Blues because of their soft and gentle demeanor and the magical sparkle in their eyes. Their graceful presence has the same calming effect on people as a blue sky, a rainbow, or ocean waves. Many people understandably are attracted to Blues, because they sense that Blues are genuinely interested in them. Although Blues represent only ten percent of the total population, they exert a tremendous influence on the minds and hearts of other people.

One of their greatest gifts is the phenomenal ability to love another person unconditionally — as much as is humanly possible. Many say that Blues are the least judgmental of all; people feel accepted by them and thrive in their presence. Blues focus on what is special about others, they are verbally affirming, and everyone is good in their eyes until proven otherwise.

When Blues speak, they often communicate from their hearts rather than their heads. In other words, they talk about their emotions and how they "feel" about things. Blues are sensitive and need to express how they feel, which can be misconstrued as a weakness by those who don't appreciate sensitivity. In fact, Blues may think their sensitivity is a curse until they realize the strength inherent in who they are. Because of the Blues' sensitivity, other people come to them when they're hurting. Accepting their sensitivity can liberate Blue men and Blue women from the pain of trying to suppress it.

Because Blues tend to take everything personally, they must be careful not to let their sensitivity cause them unnecessary anguish. Even when someone tells them not to take something personally, they may take that statement personally as well. It is difficult for Blues to separate their feelings from anyone or anything that concerns them. They don't take criticism or rejection well. They "wear their hearts on their sleeves." Tears come as easily when they're happy as when they're sad, yet people need not feel sorry for Blues or think they are fragile. If they didn't have such incredible strength, others wouldn't come to them with their problems.

John is a nice guy who loves people and will do anything to help someone in need. But lately he has had difficulty showing his gentle side to others because he has been misunderstood so often. "Sometimes guys think I'm gay or women take advantage of my kindness." John tries to appear tough on the outside but admits that he is a real softy on the inside.

It doesn't mean that a man is weak or a woman is a pushover if they are sensitive and care about others. To the contrary, it comes naturally for them to want to help other people. Helping others is enjoyable and builds Blues' self-esteem. They will help in any way they can, but their preference is to help others with their emotional needs. Helping people feel better about who they are is more rewarding than assisting with physical needs.

Of course, there is always the possibility of becoming co-dependent, and Blues have to be more careful than others. Otherwise, their amazing strength in helping others can become a weakness in trying to rescue them. A person who is co-dependent takes care of another person's needs without taking care of his own. Such a person feels responsible for others to the point of neglecting himself. Co-dependence indicates a Blue who is out-of-esteem, not a healthy Blue.

Communication is another Blue strength. Everybody is good at something, and Blues are naturally good at interacting with others. Conversation is one of their favorite pastimes, especially if they are extroverts. Going to lunch or meeting a friend for coffee is often an excuse for a social outing — the food or coffee is secondary. Blues typically show more genuine concern for the other person than interest in talking about themselves. Conversation with a Blue will usually focus on personal topics such as happiness (or lack of it) with self and others in relationships, problems and dreams concerning career goals, and what the kids are up to. Their least favorite subjects are those like war and crime, but even these can be interesting to Blues if others discuss their feelings. Talking only about the facts will make the conversation seem empty and pointless to Blues. They will usually find a way to personalize the conversation.

Oprah Winfrey demonstrates the Blues' extraordinary ability to communicate with others. She has the awesome, innate ability to communicate with a disarming style that touches the hearts of millions of people. All those hugs and tears are real! It's no accident that Oprah is the incomparable best at what she does. She is the epitome of a self-actualized Blue who is using her sensitive, compassionate and kind nature in her work. She is a great role model of what is possible for a Blue.

Their vivacious attitude and contagious enthusiasm make Blues natural promoters. They love to motivate, encourage and inspire others. When they find something good they can't wait to tell all their friends about it. When Blues get excited about something, you know you can trust them, because they will only sell something they believe in. They usually do not like selling, but when they are genuinely excited about something, they can become top salespeople.

Intuition gives Blues the ability to know or sense what others are thinking and feeling. Some people describe this ability as a sixth sense, while others call it being "psychic." If someone is saying one thing and feeling another, Blues will be first to sense the true feelings, regardless of the smoke screen.

Blues sometimes don't have facts or data to support what they know; instead, they get a "feeling" about what is true. When they trust their intuition, they are often remarkably accurate about people and situations in ways that cannot otherwise be explained. Examples of this ability are knowing who is calling before answering the phone, having a dream about someone dying before they die, or seeing something happen that they already knew would happen.

Blues must be careful not to put themselves in situations where there is a lot of disharmony because their real strength will not surface. Blue children who live in homes where there is a lot of yelling and screaming are extremely vulnerable to the negative effects of their environment, both emotionally and physically.

Blue adults will be uncomfortable where there is a lot of emotional tension and venting of hostile feelings. In a heated staff meeting, for example, a Blue might not utter a word the whole time. A Blue would be more comfortable and more likely to talk about his feelings after the meeting to figure out a more harmonious way of solving problems.

Peace and harmony are important enough to Blues that they will try to create and maintain these values at all costs. At home and in the office, Blues are the ones who want everyone to get along and be happy. Because they don't like to argue, they may appear to be cowards in a hostile situation; but their strength lies in knowing that there is a better way to resolve conflict. Blues are lovers, not fighters. They would rather walk away from a fight than engage in shouting or putting other people down.

When conflict occurs, Blues may shut down and lose their ability to communicate because they are feeling so many emotions. It is difficult for them to sort out their feelings in a hostile environment. They would rather say nothing than be embarrassed by overreacting in front of others. Most of the time, they are better off leaving the situation to go someplace quiet where they can think more clearly. They are far better communicators when there isn't a lot of emotional charge on the topic.

Mother Teresa was a good example of the Blue trait of loving, not fighting. Like other Blues, serving people gave her great joy. She considered herself the happiest nun in the world, called by God to help the poor. She went to the streets of Calcutta to live among and serve the poorest of the poor. Typical of Blues, Mother Teresa was concerned about making a difference in the lives of individuals. In her book *My Life for the Poor*, she says, "I know that there are thousands and thousands of poor, but I think of only one at a time. I can save only one at a time."

All colors loved Mother Teresa for her great concern for mankind, but for Blues she was a great role model for their values of compassion, love and concern for those who are suffering. Like Mother Teresa, Blues want to give people hope.

Blue Goals and Ideals

Blues do not strive for power or control. Instead, they have an uncompromising dedication to helping others feel good about themselves. Helping is what they most enjoy, even if they are not paid to do it. To raise a person's self-esteem or help someone reach a goal gives a Blue more personal satisfaction than money could ever buy. Money is seen as a tool to achieve ideals rather than a way to gain power or status, or impress other people.

As sensitive, caring, and compassionate individuals, Blues constantly take care of other people. They want everyone to feel loved and accepted, and they are usually the first to reach out and help someone else in need. Because they are good listeners, others come to them for comfort or advice. Blues can be trusted to be there in time of need, which is why they make good counselors and ministers. They don't mind giving their time and energy to listen to others' problems and make them feel better. To a Blue, the person with the problem isn't the only one benefiting, because Blues derive much of their own self-esteem from helping. When they make other people feel better, they share the experience of their good feelings.

A common theme in the lives of Blues is to love and be loved. In fact, they give love so freely that they usually have an abundance of friends and family members who love them. People sense their genuineness and they win friends easily — without even trying. In the words of Ralph Waldo Emerson, "Love and you shall be loved...all mankind loves a lover." This could be a motto for Blues, as witnessed by the way they live.

Many Blues are very spiritual. I have never met a Blue who is an atheist. They say that they intuitively know there is a God or a higher power, and some say they have had direct experiences in feeling this presence around them. They may belong to an established church, or practice communion with God through direct methods such as meditation or prayer.

What is important to them is to have a spiritual life, one that honors that invisible part of who they are. They feel connected with a power greater than themselves, which keeps them focused on their identity. Without this communion, Blues say they feel something is missing that is needed to give meaning to their lives.

A Blue's highest and most magnificent ideal is to make a difference in the world by improving the lives of other people. We typically see them involved in movements that promote such things as self-esteem, peace, or the process of eliminating hunger. Blues have great compassion for people and they see unlimited possibilities in them that others may not see — mostly because they look for the good in everyone. They are not snobs. Others may think they are rather naive, but the possibility of a homeless person becoming a great political leader is not unfathomable to them; he or she is only a diamond in the rough. To Blues, it is what is inside a person that counts. They will take the time to get inside and find out who a person really is, beginning with a warm smile that says, "You're okay."

Clothing and feeding a person may not give Blues as much joy as making that person believe he is unquestionably capable of taking care of himself. Their goal is to change how a person feels about himself. When one has self-respect and self-esteem, he is capable of achieving his own goals. Blues believe that the greatest secret to changing the world is first to teach people what is good about themselves, then show them how to use their glorious talents to make a contribution to others.

Not only do Blues want to see others reach their highest potential, personal growth is a primary mission in their own lives as well. Life must have meaning and purpose, and without it they experience an emptiness and feel a void inside. Working every day just to pay the bills would feel like psychic death to a Blue. The questions "Who am I?" and "Why am I here?" are typical of a Blue. Blues are likely to be found in the self-help section of bookstores, because they seem to feel the need to figure out who they are. Blues are attracted to workshops that promise self-improvement in all areas of their lives, especially relationships. By understanding themselves better, they can reach their ultimate goal — self-actualization.

To Blues, there is nothing more important than becoming the best people they can be. They hunger to be unique and despise being ordinary or like everybody else. Being exceptional allows Blues to motivate and inspire others to be their best. Blues practice what they preach and walk their talk — they don't make good phonies. Blues are on a mission to make a contribution to society. Although Blues may never quite feel like they have arrived, they live their lives committed to their purpose.

The Blue Woman

The Blue Woman is the epitome of fantastic femininity, expressed in her warmth, kindness and compassion. She may be the one who coordinates the social events at work, plans a baby shower for a friend, or tries out for cheerleader in high school. She is as popular among men as she is with family and friends. Most find her incredibly approachable and astoundingly likable, though some may think all her niceness must be fake. The truth is, she is genuinely interested in other people and others enjoy her magnificent company.

Her fashionable style makes her stand out in a crowd. She is innovative and has a flair for coordinating colors and accessories. Even if she can't afford expensive clothes they will still be in good taste. Her look will be uniquely her own. She may be attracted to bright colors but she also has an appreciation for the classic look of basic black. It is rare to find a Blue woman who doesn't like clothes. In fact, shopping is often a favorite pastime for a Blue woman. Second only to the Orange woman, she is the next most likely to shop until she drops.

What a fabulous social butterfly she is! No one can carry a social gathering quite like she can with her natural ease and grace as a hostess. People feel so comfortable in her company that it's easy for others to relax and have a good time. You can always count on the Blue woman to ensure that everyone is having fun and you can also expect to be introduced to everyone at the party. After all, lively conversation is the sign of a good time. There will be lots of hugs as she greets her guests. She will be the first to compliment others, and her sincerity will shine through. She always looks for — and often finds — the good in others.

A Blue woman's femininity and charm attract men like a magnet because she makes them feel safe and non-threatened. She is probably not the kind of woman who goes lacking for dates. In fact, her problem may be one of having too many choices and having to turn some away. Saying "no" isn't easy because she doesn't want to hurt anyone's feelings. Being assertive is one of her major challenges. The one who wins her heart must be prepared for romance. One-night stands don't appeal to her. She is looking for love, not just sex. For her, sex is empty without love. She wants to be held, hugged and cuddled, and there needs to be a bonding in the relationship first for her to trust her sexual partner. She also needs to know that she is special and that her partner really cares about her. Because she doesn't take rejection well, she will be careful to protect her feelings. Lovemaking is a deep, emotional experience for her; love, sex and romance become synonymous when she feels safe.

Exciting romance carries over into marriage as she dreams of living happily ever after. Her husband will be the center of her attention and everything else will play second fiddle in her life in the early stages of the relationship. She won't see his flaws and, quite frankly, she doesn't want to. She wants the dream of a perfect love — one where she relates to him mentally, spiritually and emotionally, as well as physically.

Supporting her mate in reaching his own exciting goals comes naturally to her. When things don't go well at the office, she will be the first to sympathize and lend an ear, and she will not take advantage of his vulnerability by being critical of him at that moment. Instead, she will take the opportunity to build his self-esteem by reminding him what an exceptionally fabulous person he is.

She doesn't expect favors in return for her good deeds, but it is not wise for him to forget her birthday or anniversary. These occasions have sentimental meaning to her and it's not too much to ask to keep her in her naturally good spirits.

Her extreme emotions can surprise her partner. Crying comes as naturally when things are good as it does when things are not. The Blue woman is the one sniffling at a romantic scene in a movie, or crying at weddings and funerals. A love song on the radio can also make her cry. She may even cry when she sees a dead animal on the road. She feels and she feels deeply. It is difficult for her to hold back these feelings, so she will usually express them.

A Blue friend of mine, whose father was becoming weaker and emotionally unstable with Parkinson's disease, went to talk to another Blue woman. As she was telling her story, she looked up to see her friend drenched in tears. Although the other woman had never met my friend's father, she empathized to the point of experiencing my friend's pain. This behavior is not unusual for a Blue woman.

The Blue woman is a loving mother who nurtures her children to bring out the best in them. She knows the importance of high self-esteem and she will strive to encourage her children. She will see and appreciate what is unique and special in each one. More likely, she will not see their flaws, which can cause discipline problems.

Discipline is not easy for her. She is more concerned with keeping peace and harmony among family members, and disciplining the children can create too much disharmony. Sometimes she may ignore the problem and hope it will go away. She does not like to resort to hitting or yelling and screaming. If she does stoop to this emotionally draining behavior, she feels extremely bad and remorseful later. Her ideal way of disciplining is to take a more democratic approach. It is more appealing for her to talk things over with her children and come to some kind of workable agreement — one that brings harmony for everybody.

Work provides her with an outlet to seek her own personal identity and interact with others. She is drawn to careers that use her talents in communication and helping others, but which also promote her own growth in reaching her potential. She will eagerly attend conferences, workshops and classes that relate to her professional growth. It is important for her to continue to grow and not become bored or outdated in her work.

She may prefer to stay home because of young children, but she will not stop growing. She will find other outlets for her growth like reading, taking classes or attending seminars. She may also become actively involved in church, volunteer for the PTA, or join women's groups for support and growth.

The Blue Man

The Blue Man is extremely kind and considerate, with a big heart, but if you're looking for someone rich he may not be your man. Not to say he cannot become rich, but he isn't motivated by money as much as other men are. A Blue man doesn't have the strong drive for power of a Green man or the competitive spirit of an Orange man. Neither does he have the strong security needs of the Gold man that motivate him to earn and save a large amount of money. The exception might be a Blue-Orange man, whose more competitive spirit would channel his creativity into fields like entertainment or communications.

Another reason for the Blue man not to be rich is that many of the attractive careers are in education and social services. Wealth is not his primary motive, but to the extent that it's important, the key would be to get rich doing something he loves. Like everything else, his work must have deep meaning. His motivation comes from his sense of service and making a contribution to others.

The trade-off for his partner will be a warm, sensitive, loving man who will support her in achieving her goals.

When he falls in love, he likes to wine and dine and shower his partner with lots of affection. He is a hopeless romantic, which some women may find smothering. Not to worry. Plenty of women want this kind of attention from their lover, and the Blue man does it naturally. He is an incredibly passionate man who likes to express his love openly. It's not unusual for him to write his partner a heartfelt poem or serenade her in a romantic moment. The Blue man feels the kind of passionate love that Romeo felt for Juliet.

The Blue man is exceptional at bringing out the best in others. Most people flourish around him, and his partner will benefit from his desire to help her reach her goals. He is not the type of man who will hold her back from improving herself or be intimidated by her success. In fact, the happier she is with herself, the more attractive she will be to him. The only danger is that if she doesn't have quality time with him, he could get upset. He needs lots of attention.

The partner of a Blue man must remind him often that she loves him. His continual need for reassurance doesn't mean that he is insecure. He just needs to hear that he is loved. He doesn't want to have to figure it out, he wants it said explicitly. After all, he thrives on good, clear communication.

Marriage has special meaning, and he is more than willing to do his share to make the relationship work. In fact, he will go the extra mile for his partner because giving to others comes easily to him. He is also not afraid to open up and let his partner touch the soft part of his heart, as long as she makes it safe for him. He only needs to know that he can trust her to validate his feelings. In other words, he doesn't want to be made to feel wrong or stupid for having whatever feelings he has. He needs to be able to express his honest emotions with his partner.

Be prepared to share him with others (not in a romantic way, of course) because like his Blue female counterpart he will be popular. Other people enjoy his company and want to spend time with him. He is good at nurturing others, and his friends like to talk to him when they need someone to listen. The Blue man's need to interact with others is as much a part of who he is as his fingerprints.

As a father, he will be attentive to his children. Family relationships are important to him and he will make time to spend with his kids. He will feel emotionally bonded with them, and they will feel that they can talk openly to him. They will think of him as a friend as well as a father.

He has to be careful not to be overly permissive with his children. He wants to please them and make them happy, and they can take advantage of his good heart. Like the Blue woman, he will have to work harder at setting limits and disciplining his children.

If he is Blue-Orange, he will be more playful with his children since his Orange influence makes him playful by nature. It is not unusual to see him leave the adult conversation and go off to play with the children. Like his children, he knows how to have fun.

Blue Children

Blue children are incredibly soft and cuddly babies who seek lots of attention from the beginning. The more extroverted ones will be especially demanding of your time. They don't like to be left alone. A Blue baby is sensitive and will learn to respond to your emotions early. Sometimes it's hard for them to distinguish between their feelings and those of others. They may cry because other children are crying or scream when other children scream. Unlike other children who mimic each other, Blue children tend to experience whatever emotion they are expressing.

Blue children have a natural gift for language and will usually talk early. The more extroverted ones will talk a lot and will probably talk to themselves when no one else will listen. Because of their honesty, their lack of discretion about what to say and what not to say can sometimes be embarrassing — like giving away family secrets. Introverts will not talk as much, especially around strangers. In fact, they may need a little encouragement to talk to other people, but remember not to try to make them extroverts. They will never be as talkative as extroverted children.

I cannot overstate how important it is for Blue children to know they are loved and valued. They will flourish in an atmosphere where love is expressed. Other children need to know they are loved, but it needs to be explicit with Blue children. They need to hear the words "I love you." Physical touch is equally important. They thrive on hugs, kisses, holding hands, and pats on the back, and they need this reassurance daily. If they are punished, they especially need to be reminded that they are still loved. Otherwise, punishment to them could mean they are not loved. Remember, they are sensitive children. If it is hard to believe how important this is to these children, try expressing your love in this way for a week and be prepared to see the incredible difference.

These children have great imaginations, which show up early in their ability to make up stories. They may talk about friends whom you know they don't have, or they may assign personalities to their stuffed animals, dolls or live pets. Friends may exist only in their imaginations, but nevertheless seem real to them. Don't stifle this imagination and don't worry that they will grow up to be big liars. Imagination will be an important asset for them as they mature. The more you read to them, the more you will foster it.

School has special meaning for Blue children because they love to learn. They will be excited to discover more opportunities for imagination, but they may also have a tendency to daydream, especially if they are bored. They usually do well in subjects like reading, writing and spelling, or those that deal with people, such as social studies.

Teachers play a special role in Blue children's lives. They set the tone that either motivates these children to open up and learn or shut down and withdraw. It is helpful for teachers to know their names and acknowledge them. Because these kids like to please others, they will work hard not to disappoint their teachers. They may offer to help at recess and after school, because they are seeking a relationship with the teacher. Positive feedback is necessary to these children's well-being.

Blue children will be unusually popular among their peers. They have a lot of compassion for others and won't say hurtful things to other children. In fact, when others are hurt or embarrassed, these children will have a lot of empathy and be the first to try to make them feel better. They love to give from their hearts and they may give away valuable possessions to dear friends or people they care about deeply. Don't worry, they aren't trying to buy friends. They don't have to — they make friends too easily. Instead, gift-giving is their way of expressing their deep love and appreciation for the friendship.

Blue children will have to be careful not to let their popularity interfere with school. They love to talk to others and others enjoy talking to them. They may be tempted to talk inappropriately in the classroom. If anything gets them in trouble, it's likely to be this. But this is about as bad as it gets, because they are not fighters or the ones who pick on other children. When I was in school, teachers used to make the extroverted Blue kids write "I will not talk in class" one hundred times.

When there is conflict with the teacher, Blue children may have the strongest reaction. They may withdraw or even give up. It's not unusual for them to think "Nobody cares," or "What's the use of trying?" They identify so strongly with their teacher that they have a hard time separating their feelings about the teacher from their achievement in the classroom. If they feel the teacher is rejecting them, their love for that teacher may even turn to hate. It is difficult for them to express their anger, and they will probably keep these feelings bottled up inside and put distance between themselves and the teacher. The teacher needs to understand the sensitivity of Blue children. A little TLC and some positive strokes are all it takes to turn them around.

Blue Out-of-Esteem Behavior

Like everyone, when Blues are out-of-esteem, their strengths become their weaknesses. People whom they would otherwise enjoy being with and helping can become their biggest stressor. Blues can feel so depressed and overwhelmed by their own emotions that they are incapable of listening to other people's problems. When this happens they have a tendency to withdraw and wallow in self-pity. One of their greatest fears is to be alone or unloved, so take heed when a Blue resorts to withdrawing from other people. Many Blues will say they spend a lot of time crying and indulging in overeating when they are not happy.

Although they love being available for others who need them, they may feel embarrassed to let others know when they are hurting. Because Blues normally are strong and supportive, it's easy to forget they sometimes need help and support themselves, unless they ask for it. Blues must be careful not to use passive-aggressive behavior to get what they want from others. One example of passive-aggressive behavior is punishing others by giving them the silent treatment or ignoring them.

Blues may react to their own problems by becoming overly involved in helping others. Someone else's problems can become the main focus, even to the point of being an emotional burden. This is why it is so easy for them to become the ultimate rescuers. They must remember that taking care of themselves and not suppressing their own feelings gives them the strength they need to be emotionally available to help others.

Blues usually have a hard time saying no, but when they are feeling vulnerable it is even more difficult for them. They can be too nice and act like a doormat. At work, they might agree to take on too many responsibilities. They may go along with friends even when what others want to do isn't appealing. I know a Blue woman who went with her friends every week to a restaurant that she hated. When I asked her why, she said she was afraid they wouldn't like her if she didn't go with them. It is not unusual for Blues to think that if they say no, others will not like them or they will hurt some one else's feelings.

It is not uncommon for Blue children who are out-of-esteem to resort to the "perfect child syndrome." They will try to do everything perfectly right to please those around them. They can be hurting tremendously on the inside but smile and pretend to be happy. They will shut down and suppress all of their emotions to avoid being sensitive and vulnerable to others. Of course, the danger is that they will have a hard time recovering these emotions later in life, and this can cause them great pain and loss of identity. They may learn to fear one of their greatest gifts — their ability to be sensitive to other people.

6

The Green Personality — Knowledge Is Power

‹ ‹ ‹ ‹ ‹ ‹ ‹ ‹ ‹ ‹ ‹ ‹ › › › › › › › › › › › ›

Greens are the exceptionally deep and brilliant thinkers of the world. When describing Greens, others typically use words like "intelligent," "clever," "wise," and "witty." They are remembered as the ones who got the better grades in school, and they often rise to leadership roles.

Like Blues, the Greens represent a small percentage (approximately ten percent) of the population, but the two groups are otherwise very different. Unlike the sociable Blues, you won't find a Green hanging out at parties or any other social gatherings. Mundane conversations and small talk are extremely boring to Greens. They are more likely to be found in loftier places: an art museum; a lecture, class or seminar; the theater; or the library. They prefer intellectually stimulating environments with like-minded people. They are not necessarily snobs. They simply don't find idle chit-chat interesting, and they probably don't do it well either. As a matter of fact, they don't like participating in anything they aren't good at.

As perfectionists, Greens have a strong need to be competent at any endeavor they deem important. They will invest all their time and energy in doing something right or not at all, which often causes them to be their own worst critics.

Greens place high standards not only on themselves but on others as well. Unfortunately, others seldom live up to their expectations. Many people say they feel intellectually inadequate around Greens.

To Greens, knowledge is power, and their insatiable thirst for knowledge is what drives them. This behavior can be observed in scientists, who typically are Green. The university professor who is paid to acquire knowledge continually through research is also an example of this personality. Research and development is an ideal career for some Greens. Greens like being acknowledged for their above-average intellectual ability. Typically they score higher on IQ exams than others, which reflects the value they place on information and knowledge. Mensa, the organization for those with high IQs, is heavily populated with Greens.

Greens have such an astonishingly broad base of information that they usually know something about almost any subject. Whatever the topic, they think globally — the bigger the idea, the better. They are more likely to express a global perspective than one that relates only to them or the people they know. Unlike Blues, they don't focus their attention on individuals. They are objective thinkers who need to know the theory or the principle behind any concept and detest simplistic explanations.

They also tend to be out of touch with the more mundane things in life, which simply aren't interesting to them. A Green woman I know says she has a difficult time relating to the typical conversations of some of the women she knows. According to her, "These women will often talk about shopping for fashionable clothes or preparing their favorite recipes, or share their opinions about favorite television shows. While I like to be informed, I find these conversations to be too ordinary and extremely boring."

Whoever said "ignorance is bliss" was obviously not a Green. To Greens, ignorance is a curse. To be ignorant is to be uninformed, and to be uninformed is to be stupid. Greens consistently say they cannot tolerate stupidity in themselves or others and this is one of their biggest causes of stress from other people. If asked a question they cannot answer, they are more apt to say, "I don't know" or "I'd have to look into that," than to risk an answer that might sound uninformed or stupid. Their language is precise and focused. Repetition and redundancy are a real turn-off, so others had better catch it the first time because Greens are unlikely to repeat themselves. Some of them say they cannot even give the same speech twice because they get bored with the repetition.

Like Bill Gates, co-founder of the largest software company in the world and the youngest self-made billionaire in America, Greens have the ability to be phenomenal problem-solvers. Unlike the Oranges, who prefer a physical challenge, Greens love a mental challenge. Solving a puzzle, winning a game of chess, or unraveling a mystery appeals to them. The joy of discovering a solution to a problem is equivalent to the rush an Orange might get from bungee jumping.

Greens tend to get restless; once they've mastered the challenge or solved the problem, they are ready to move on to something else. Great thinkers like Einstein, Aristotle and Plato all had this kind of mind.

Of course, someone doesn't have to be famous to be Green. The person sitting next to you in the office, a family member, or a friend could also be a Green. The one who asks the most questions is most likely Green.

Opposition does not intimidate them. Unlike Blues, who will avoid arguments, Greens think of them as a challenge, which makes them good debaters and negotiators. They have the remarkable ability to analyze everything. Picking ideas apart and putting them back together again is their unusual way of having fun. Their tremendous curiosity drives them to want to have a thorough understanding of something they are interested in. The way they sort the True Colors cards is a good example. They usually spend more time with the cards than anyone else because of their need to think before they can respond. It's not unusual for Greens to relate to something on each card and to think that no single color represents them more than another. I usually respond by saying, "I understand your response, because human beings have a multitude of values in common, but what I'm looking for is your preference for certain values over others." Usually after a lengthy discussion and giving of examples they will choose the Green card as their primary color. I now anticipate this response from Greens because it happens so often.

Greens are incredibly self-assured, confident about who they are, and not easily influenced by the opinions of others. In the workplace, it means little that someone has a title or some authority. Greens are only impressed if someone is competent at what he does and lives up to his title. Greens don't thrive on positive feedback to the extent that Blues do, because to them, if something is positive and true it's also obvious, so why say it? Besides, Greens are the final judges of how accurate any feedback is. Their perfectionism makes it difficult for anything ever to be quite good enough, but by the same token, insults don't bother them very much. They will always consider the source and decide the truth for themselves.

If complimented, Greens may say, "I know," which may be perceived as arrogance, but they are merely telling the truth. If a Green compliments you — cherish it. They don't say things just to make people feel good. In fact, it's not easy to get a compliment out of Greens. Sensitive people had better not ask for opinions or advice from Greens because they'll tell the truth, like it or not.

The key to making an effective compliment to Greens is the content itself. Complimenting their appearance will not have the same impact that it will on a Blue or Orange. To make an effective compliment to Greens, tell them how intelligent they are or how impressed you are with their ingenuity in some area. This kind of compliment will get their attention and it will be meaningful.

Be careful what you criticize. If you tell Greens that their social graces leave something to be desired, you probably won't get a rise out of them. They may even ignore you. But if you criticize them for their ideas or their work, you should be prepared for a verbal fight. They will defend their ideas and their work to the end, and they do not like to be wrong. A woman I know had never seen her husband get angry about anything in the ten years they were married. Then one day, while they were out with a group of friends, one of them responded to something her husband said by calling it a stupid idea.

It is rare to see Greens become emotional in public. They feel too embarrassed to behave this way, and many of them say to cry in public would be a sign of weakness. Being emotional means being out of control, a feeling they detest. Instead they maintain a cool, calm, and collected composure and often wear blank expressions — especially the more introverted Greens. Being very complex, they can be difficult to read. Unlike Blues, they know how to keep their emotions under a lid and use their well-trained, logical minds. Even if they are excited about something, they won't jump up and down to express their excitement. The exception might be a Green-Blue blend. Green-Blues vacillate between stoicism and acting like an emotional Blue, but underneath you will find a Green very much under control emotionally.

Striving to be the most popular among friends is not a Green goal. Wanting to be liked is more of a Blue characteristic. Greens seek quality in friendship and usually settle for a few close friends. It's not easy for them to find others to whom they can relate, so they sometimes feel isolated and different from those around them. At work, they may spend time talking to only one or two people. A small percentage of Greens are extroverts, and because so many of them are introverts, they often are described as loners. When they do socialize, they prefer small groups over big parties.

Green Goals and Ideals

Greens can be amazing, self-contained think tanks. I tease some of my Green friends about being idea-a-minute people and tell them they should get paid to think. Why not? They think all the time anyway. They prefer to deal with ideas and concepts rather than tedious details. Leave the details to a Gold. One of their favorite pastimes is to dream up exciting and innovative ways of creating change. Because they are perfectionists, they always see an opportunity to improve the system, whether it is education, politics and government, or moving a company forward. Forward is their favorite direction. The status quo soon becomes frustrating and boring. Hanging on to the past or even living in the present is not nearly as exciting as thinking of the future — with their ideas incorporated, of course.

Greens, like Blues, are driven to be change agents. Whereas Blues use their great people skills and compassion to make changes in the personal lives of others, Greens use their innate leadership ability to change systems that impact the lives of many people. Voicing their opinions and fighting for what they believe in comes naturally to them. They detest injustice and will strive to change the social, political, and economic systems that determine and control the lives of the people they represent. Two contemporary examples of Greens are Gloria Steinem and Martin Luther King, Jr.

Gloria Steinem has been the most outstanding and persuasive spokesperson for the feminist movement in the United States. Author, journalist and co-founder of *Ms.* magazine, Steinem set out to fight discrimination against all women, across economic and racial boundaries. She used her writing ability to raise women's consciousness levels and to educate the public on the women's movement. Her goal was to create better opportunities for women.

Unlike Mother Teresa, who worked one-on-one with the poor, Steinem had a global focus. She chose to change social and economic systems that affected the lives of all women. Each was effective in her own way, which demonstrates how Blues prefer to make social change versus how Greens go about it.

Martin Luther King, Jr., is another example of a Green who wanted to make changes on a global scale. He dedicated his life to creating world peace and justice for all human beings by being a catalyst for social change against racism in the United States. As a Green, it was evident at an early age that he was sensitive to injustice. While in elementary school, King witnessed a confrontation his father had with a white man. He later told his mother, "When I get to be a man, I'm going to hit this thing, I'm going to hit it hard, Mother; there's no such thing as one people better than another. The Lord made us all equal, and I'm going to see to that." As a Green, King also recognized that changes had to be made in the system that governed people's lives for any real change to take place.

King came from a family line of ministers, but like other Greens, he was an intellectual. At first he considered careers in law or medicine, but he was so impressed by his college professors who were also preachers that he changed his mind about his life's work. He decided that the ministry could be intellectually meaningful as well as emotionally inspiring. He then chose an intellectual African-American congregation in the South that became a direct means of social change for his people. When his father said, "You won't make any money preaching," King's response reflected the Green characteristic of not allowing materialism to compromise a higher value. He said, "I'll preach for nothing. I'm not going to worry about money."

King was inspired by another Green intellectual. While in college, he heard a lecture on Mahatma Gandhi that changed his life. He had admired Gandhi but thought he was an impractical idealist. When he realized that Gandhi had liberated India from British rule without violence and caused political and social change through the power of love, King adopted this method of passive resistance to fight against white racism in America. Knowledge became the catalyst for action.

Their work gives Greens much of their self-esteem. Some would characterize them as all work and no play. When they set their minds to something, they will strive to be the best at it. This is why they often rise to the top in organizations. Their thinking is ahead of most people's, and they are not shy about voicing their opinions.

The Green Woman

The Green woman is the most self-sufficient and independent of all females, and she will insist on having her freedom. In fact, she is not the type of woman who is satisfied to be a stay-at-home wife or mother. More than likely, she will find it difficult to give up her career goals, because home is seldom enough to satisfy all of her interests. Because she is a Green, she may believe that anything a man can do she can do better. Her man will have to understand and appreciate her need not to feel restricted.

While bright colors and trendy fashions are more attractive to Blue and Orange women, the Green woman's tasteful style is more conservative. She prefers a classic and sophisticated look.

Romancing her can be quite a challenge. She prefers men who have it all — ambition, strength, good looks and intelligence — which is not too much to ask of the man who deserves her. She is intrigued by men who have enough softness to balance her strong personality, yet her tendency to be domineering could cause her to take the lead in the relationship. She could be a threat to a man who has a problem with strong-willed women.

She has strong convictions, and others sometimes resent her because she can be outspoken. She is sometimes labeled "the bitch," but she isn't concerned about what others think. She tends to be honest and direct about what she says — sometimes brutally honest — but others always know where they stand with her because she is not wishy-washy. Her friends understand her, because she is selective about who they are; they must be worthy companions with intelligence equal to or higher than hers.

Her choice of careers must be challenging, and because she likes to be the boss, she will probably rise to the top of her organization. Taking orders from someone else is not her cup of tea. She is most likely to go into male-dominated careers like medicine, law and corporate management. Besides being outspoken, she is brave and not at all intimidated by men.

A Green women takes her work seriously and is very focused. She may appear aloof and unfriendly because she doesn't want to be part of a social club on the job. Small talk with her colleagues or taking coffee breaks together doesn't appeal to her. It is difficult for her to relate to office gossip. In fact, she thinks it's a complete waste of time. Professionally she is focused on her competence — her outstanding ability to do her job well. She admits to perfectionism and has high expectations of others.

While other girls were playing with dolls and fantasizing about being mommies and wives, she was probably preparing for and dreaming about her wonderful future career. In some ways she is the most misunderstood of all women because she does not always play the traditional female role. Blue women thrive on love and romance and find relationships to be an important part of their lives. Gold women look forward to getting married and raising a family as part of their social responsibility. Green women are more like Orange women, needing to be independent.

While Orange women want their independence in order to be able to do as they please and not answer to anyone, a Green woman's need for independence is motivated by her desire to use her intellect to achieve her goals. She probably got good grades in school and knows she is capable of going into any career she chooses. Sometimes she will put so much emphasis on her career that she doesn't put much energy into love relationships. Many Green women postpone marriage until their career goals are set.

As a wife and mother, she will perform her duties well, even the things she may not like, such as housework. If she can afford it, she will probably have a housekeeper. She may tend to put her husband on a pedestal and expect him to be perfect, but she won't mind taking on the role of partner in helping him achieve his dreams. She will have high expectations of her children as well, and will teach them to be independent. She probably won't fuss over them or be overly protective, and she may have to work on expressing her love in a tender and demonstrative way, especially if her children are other personality types.

The Green Man

The Green man is ideal for a woman attracted to highly intelligent men who are ambitious about achieving their career goals. He seems destined to be a leader, so a partner must be prepared to let him do what it takes to excel in his career. Many Green men end up being leaders in politics, education, business and the entertainment industry. Whatever organization they choose, their clever ideas and ability to articulate them bring recognition.

Work has a high priority in a Green man's life. Although much of his identity is tied up in his endeavors, his partner needn't be put off or take it personally. He simply thinks he must be a leader. It is difficult for him to work for someone else and be told what to do, and he is impatient with others who are slower.

He may need to be reminded to balance his professional and personal lives. His partner can't assume that he sees this need. Many of my friends who are married to Green men tell me that balance is one of the major challenges in their relationship. Fortunately, if the Green man respects his partner enough to be with her, he also will value her opinions — but she will have to speak up with them. Like his female counterpart, it is easy for the Green man to lose touch with the mundane details of everyday living.

Because opposites attract, he may be especially intrigued by women who are soft and feminine. This kind of woman makes him feel secure in his masculinity and able to be the initiator and leader in the relationship.

The secret to keeping him interested is to give him freedom to pursue his goals. He doesn't find clinging vines attractive, and he will expect his partner to be independent and intelligent, with a life of her own. She cannot expect to dictate to him or control him, because he will never stand for it. In fact, he may lose interest in the relationship. Supporting his partner's career goals is not a problem as long as she supports his.

He will set high standards for his children, whom he will expect to earn good grades in school. Of course, the only good grade to him is an A. His partner may need to help him appreciate the special talents of each child, especially those who are not academically strong. He will need to see his children as individuals who have different strengths that are equally important. Whatever they do, he will expect them to excel. It is critical for him to give the kids a chance to shine individually by allowing them to do what comes naturally to them. By helping his children figure out their true colors, he can have a better understanding of what each child's natural strengths and talents are.

Green Children

Parents of Green children have their work cut out for them, not because their children are like active Orange children (although Green children can be active), but because Green children are very independent and have minds of their own. Their strong wills can be detected early as they defy rules that other kids accept. They can't be expected to be as obedient as Gold children or to have a strong need to please like Blue children. The difference between Green children and other two-year-olds is that Greens never quite outgrow the need to say no. Sometimes, however, after they have had a chance to think things through (their favorite pastime), they may change their minds and adopt ideas as their own. Because these children know what they want, be careful not to impose your will on them. Thoughtless scolding that lacks a logical explanation is useless with them. They need to understand and they want things to make sense, so be prepared to explain a lot to these children. The payoff will be respect and obedience when your rules make logical sense.

Green children have a natural curiosity about everything in life. Encourage it — the knowledge they are storing will pay off later. They are often brilliant and need a lot of mental stimulation at home and at school. Many can figure out a puzzle better and more quickly than most adults. A Green child's mind is his greatest strength, so cherish it and help him channel his creative energy.

Green children usually love school and thrive on learning, but unless the teacher understands them they may prove to be the most challenging children in the class. They probably won't be hyperactive or present a discipline problem, but they may question the teacher to keep themselves mentally stimulated. Because they catch on quickly and are ready to move on before other children, they may need projects and extra assignments to keep them on track. Otherwise they may daydream or become bored to the point of losing interest in school. The teacher may be put off by the Green child's constant need to ask "why," but should be prepared to give more than a superficial answer. Faking it or not giving a good answer will undermine the Green child's respect for the teacher. Parents and teachers would do well to equip the Green child to research and find answers for himself.

Green children will probably need help learning social graces. They can be direct and sarcastic and hurt other kids without realizing what they are doing. They are not naturally sensitive people and they can be out of touch with how they come across to others. Some Green kids are so awkward socially and so focused on their intellect that they define the term "nerd." Instead of isolating themselves, however, Green children need to use their mental ability to learn how to communicate with others.

Greens have a strong desire to be the best at whatever they are interested in. Science may fascinate them, or they may be artistic, and some will enjoy figuring out complicated math problems. Things that boggle the minds of other children become an intriguing challenge to Greens. They will strive to earn A's in their classes and will not be satisfied with anything less. It is not unusual for them to get depressed over a B. Class valedictorians are usually Green. Their desire to be the best will carry over into their careers, where they will strive to be the most competent in their chosen fields and rise to the top. They could easily end up being the presidents of their companies or the country.

Green Out-of-Esteem Behavior

The strengths that become weaknesses when Greens are out-of-esteem are their intellect and ability to communicate. Because Greens communicate from their heads rather than their hearts, when they are out-of-esteem they may resort to bitter sarcasm or cynicism. Their clever use of words can become a sharp weapon that penetrates the heart or cuts through to the bone. You may think that only sticks and stones can break bones, but the words of an out-of-esteem Green can break the spirit. A broken spirit is difficult to recover, which is why it is dangerous to be out-of-esteem. Adults have told me some horrendous things said to them as children that they never forgot. Worse still, many believed what they were told, because they were children and didn't know any better. I don't mean to imply that only Greens say cruel things. My point is that Greens have such a great command of the language that their words are powerful, and they need to be sensitive to how they can affect other people.

Another weakness for Greens is being so analytical that they become indecisive and immobilized by their own thoughts. Every good reason can have an equal and opposite bad reason, to the point where thinking turns into an obsession. Some Greens say that sometimes they literally cannot think of anything else until a thought is resolved in their own minds. Their vision may become so myopic that they feel stuck until they solve the problem. The best way for Greens to break this cycle is to take action.

Greens are such perfectionists that they can become highly critical of themselves and others. Nothing is ever quite good enough. Greens can become impatient with the lack of equal ability in other people. Although it is difficult, Greens must learn to be more patient with themselves and others. No human being is perfect — everyone makes mistakes. It's okay to be wrong sometimes.

7

The Gold Personality — Plan It

Everyone knows someone who is Gold, because Golds represent almost half the population. Recognizing them is easy, but not because they have a gregarious nature or wear flashy clothes. Golds are usually quiet and more conservative than other types. One can expect Golds to be neat, clean, well-groomed and dressed appropriately for the occasion. Unlike the Oranges, they don't desire to stand out and be noticed in a crowd.

If you want something done, give it to a Gold. They are dependable and reliable and can be counted on to do what they say and be where they are supposed to be in a timely manner. If they say they will meet you at eight o'clock, they mean eight o'clock sharp — not five after eight. Punctuality is important to them. In fact, arriving early to make sure they are not late is not unusual.

Betty expresses classic Gold behavior. She is usually the first to arrive at work, family gatherings or lunch meetings with friends. She says, "I have my clocks at home and in my car set ten minutes fast to make sure that I am never late." She has been known to leave friends behind if they are not ready on time.

When asked why she is so obsessed with being on time, Betty replies, "I just hate being late. Besides, I might miss something."

Being late is so stressful that some Golds say they would rather not go at all if it means being late. A friend of mine once told me that he is so anxious when he's running late that he begins to perspire and his heart races. He says, "There have been times when I have turned around and gone back home because I felt being late would be rude to others who were on time."

Organizing and keeping things neat and tidy are skills Golds have mastered. The home of a Gold may look like no one lives there. Everything is in its right place. The dishes are so clean you can see your reflection and the floors are spotless enough to eat off of them. Golds don't like dirt; cleanliness is next to godliness. It is difficult for Golds to sit and relax because there is always work to be done — another dish to wash or, if they have children, another toy to put away.

Proper behavior and doing things "the right way" gives them much pride. If you don't have strong opinions about right and wrong behavior, you're probably not a primary Gold. It is easier for Golds to do something themselves than to show others how to do it. They may even do a task over after someone else has done it. A young woman in one of my workshops said she learned early not to bother putting away her father's laundry, because he would refold everything the way he felt it was supposed to be, and organize the things according to color and size.

This same quality of organization applies to the workplace. If you walk into an office that belongs to a Gold, you will recognize it immediately. Everything will be in its right place, and there won't be dirt on the floor or dust on the furniture. The desk will be neat and clean with only the necessary things on it: a phone, a pen or pencil, a calendar, and probably a list of things to do. Somewhere in the office you will find family pictures, certificates, awards, trophies, and anything else that shows recognition. If there is a bookcase, the books will be lined up in an orderly way. It's not surprising to find them in alphabetical order.

I once borrowed a book from a Gold office mate and she reminded me I had not returned it. When I showed her where I had put the book back on her shelf, she said, "Well, no wonder I couldn't find it, you didn't put it back in alphabetical order." It never occurred to me that anyone, except librarians, put their books in order. Then again, I'm not a primary Gold.

The comfort of doing things in a familiar way makes Golds accustomed to repeating habitual patterns. This is how they know what is expected of them, what to do and what the results will be each time. They like their world predictable. Save the surprises for the Oranges. To others, this behavior may seem boring, but to a Gold it means stability and security.

I know a Gold who likes to park her car in the same spot every day when she comes to work. She likes to eat at the same restaurant and order the same thing on the menu. When I asked her why she does this, she said she likes knowing exactly what she will get. She's afraid that if she orders something different she will be disappointed and have her lunch ruined.

The opposite of the free-spirited Oranges, Golds are more serious by nature. They tend to be perfectionists who pay attention to the smallest detail. If there is a word misspelled on a page or the tiniest spot on a piece of clothing, they will be the first to notice. I love my Gold friends to read my manuscripts, because they always spot errors that everyone else has missed.

They also tend to worry a lot. After all, paying attention to all the details and everyone else around them creates anxiety. It is their nature to want control so that things don't go wrong, but something always does. They try to prevent things from going wrong, yet stay prepared for when things don't go as planned. What may sound like pessimism to everyone else, they call being realistic and sensible. The Boy Scout motto, "Be Prepared," is spoken like a true Gold.

Golds are cautious and methodical when it comes to making decisions. They need to know all the facts before they feel comfortable enough to make a move. They also rely on sensory experience as their major source of knowledge. In other words, to believe something is real they need to see it, hear it, taste it, touch it or smell it. They do not trust their intuition, like Blues or maybe Greens would. They are not risk-takers like Oranges either. If you want to sell them an idea or product, you must show them all the facts and convince them it is totally safe. If you don't, you can forget about selling them anything.

It is also important that things be done in an orderly and sequential way. Start with step one and progress through to step ten with Golds — do not follow any kind of reversed order. If you skip around or miss anything, you will confuse them. When they start asking you to repeat something, chances are you're either going too fast or you've left out some details. If you try to rush Golds, you will lose them and they will not trust you. You must build a solid foundation for them to make a decision by giving them all the facts, and then give them time to process the information. The good news is that when they do make up their minds, they don't tend to vacillate. They are goal-oriented people who like to think things through thoroughly, then make a decision before moving on.

Planning everything is important. To Golds, not to plan is foolish. They don't like to be caught by surprise, and planning provides the predictability that they need. My Gold friends always know in advance what they are doing on a daily basis. I've learned never to ask them to do anything at the last minute.

How do Golds keep track of all of this? Calendars, of course. Golds alone could keep a time-management company in business. To some people all this planning takes the spontaneity out of life, but Golds don't value spontaneity. They may appreciate this quality in other people, like comedians or entertainers, but they can't be that way themselves. Golds are content to let the Oranges, who do it naturally, entertain the rest of us.

When I said that Golds plan everything, I meant literally everything. I've been told that they even know in advance how they will spend their leisure time. They like to have fun like anyone else, but they will plan their fun. If they take a trip, they will start saving their money and making plans months in advance. Their trip may include a daily itinerary of scheduled things to do. Unlike Oranges, they would never hop on a plane and figure out where to stay or what to do once they've arrived. Impromptu causes stress and takes the fun out of the trip.

Because of their frugality, bargain-hunting is a necessary part of Golds' lives. I tease my Gold friends about being the first to line up for the day-after-Christmas sale to buy cards, wrapping paper, and gifts for next year. Who do you think is in line at the grocery store cashing in all those coupons clipped out of the newspaper? If you want to know where to shop for the biggest discounts in town, ask a Gold. He likes to comparison shop and talk about the good deal he got on an item. To a Gold, it is silly to pay full price for something that is cheaper someplace else. The time spent comparing prices at different stores is worth it.

Gold Goals and Ideals

A social gathering is not the best place to find Golds. Because of their strong work ethic, you may find them working late at the office. Their sense of duty and responsibility would rule out attending parties for the sake of pure fun. On the other hand, if they want to make a business contact — or they have some other practical reason that offsets the frivolity — they may do well at a party. Gold women often are the guests who help the host or hostess at a party.

Social gatherings that involve family rituals and ceremonies are preferred events for Golds, because they place a high value on family. The most traditional of the four colors, Golds like to celebrate the major holidays, births, baptisms, weddings and anniversaries with their families. These occasions are a major part of their social life, and the perfect time to bring out the best china and silver to use with the fancy tablecloth.

Planning for the future is critical, because Golds are security-conscious. Anyone can say this is important, but Golds actually do something about it. They put money away for everything from their children's college education to their retirement needs. From my conversations with Golds, I think they have more insurance policies and medical plans than anyone else. Golds are not the ones who will end up broke or counting on Social Security when they retire. In fact, they save so much of their money for retirement that some Golds say they live better than ever when they do retire. Of course, they would never spend it all. They want to leave some to their offspring. It pays to know a Gold. It took a Gold to convince me to save my own money. I've gotten better at it, but I still spend my money much too frivolously compared to a Gold.

Predictability is also reflected in their work. Many Golds tell me they like repeating the same duties every day, and when their routine is altered it throws them off. They also say they are not bothered by mundane and tedious tasks. Most important, whatever task they accomplish will be done thoroughly and efficiently. Golds do well when they know what is expected of them. They probably need the least amount of supervision because they do such a good job of monitoring themselves. At work they can be found where they are supposed to be and doing what they are supposed to be doing. They have the same expectations of others and much of their language consists of "shoulds" and "should nots."

Greens and Oranges are more likely to seek positions of leadership, and it's easier to find famous personalities for these colors. Blues and Golds are not as comfortable in leadership roles. Blues prefer to work one-on-one with people, and many avoid positions of power. Golds find more comfort in middle management positions, which, of course, puts someone else in the role of leader. The exception is in politics. Golds' concern for law and order makes politics appealing. According to David Keirsey and Ray Choinier, authors of *Presidential Temperament,* twenty of our first forty United States presidents were Gruarians, which is the Gold personality.

Gerald Ford is an example of a Gold who became president. His Gold qualities initially secured his position as vice president to Richard Nixon. Because of the condition of the country at that time, Nixon was looking for someone who was honest and loyal, and he found these qualities in Gerald Ford.

Like many Golds, Ford was drawn to politics, which became his life career. He made his way up through the ranks and worked diligently to get to the top. Ford's perpetual re-election over twenty-four years to the House of Representatives showed he had staying power. As president, like other Golds, he was conscientious and hard-working. Some accused him of being slow and plodding, but to him it was more important to be thorough and complete his tasks than to be speedy and make mistakes. His family was important to him, and he proved to be a devoted family man. As a youth, he was proud to earn Eagle Scout honors.

The slogan, "If it ain't broke, don't fix it," must have come from a Gold; Golds are status quo people who resist change. They feel threatened by any change that would upset traditional values, laws and institutions. While no society can progress without vision and change, it also needs stability to prevent chaos. Working together to utilize our strengths in the best interest of society preserves this important balance. It is the nature of the universe and everything in it to change, but Golds know that too much rapid change will throw any system off balance.

The Gold Woman

The Gold woman is strong in character and determined to have what it takes to make her happy. Because she is practical about everything, a man who can provide financial security is important to her.

She can be a social climber who prefers to be on top, with her mate bringing in the money while she takes care of the home and children. She feels it's important to have a properly run home and good supervision of her children. A Gold sister of mine said she only went to college because I pushed her. She said all she ever wanted was to get married and have children and a house with a white picket fence. After suffering a divorce, she now thanks me because her education allows her, as a single parent, to support herself and her son.

If a Gold woman stays home, she is likely to spend time with organizations that concern her children, like the PTA and Girl Scouts, or volunteer her time at her children's school. She takes seriously her role as a mother and wife and her mate's role as a father and provider for his family. Many Gold women say the adjustment to today's role as a liberated career woman has been difficult.

She will demand that her partner have good manners. She will expect him to behave properly at the dinner table, and she won't tolerate him eating sloppily or biting his fork. She will be fussy about her partner dressing neatly — shaving, a clean shirt and polished shoes are important to her. Because she pays attention to tiny details, a spot on his tie will not go unnoticed. It is her nature to have high expectations of her mate.

In spite of her sometimes annoyingly meticulous nature, the Gold woman can be quite generous. She won't mind spending long hours organizing her partner's personal life, keeping his clothes clean, and performing other wifely duties. But she may have a difficult time verbally expressing her love for him, so these things will be her way of showing her feelings. In fact, she may find herself saying, "I wouldn't do all these things for you if I didn't love you."

Because she's a firm disciplinarian, you won't see her children running around the house or the neighborhood screaming and yelling. She believes children should learn early to behave in a quiet and respectful manner. They will always be neat and clean and nicely dressed. Her children will know they can count on dinner together every night with Daddy at the head of the table. Gold men and women both believe that everyone has their place in the relationship and there should be respect for authority. Daddy's place is as the leader and the one in charge of the family. The children are expected to know this and give him his due respect. A Gold mother's firmness may leave a gap in the emotional needs of her children. If she is a Gold-Blue, she will probably be freer in expressing her love.

The Gold woman does not live in a fantasy world. Instead, she pays attention to all the realities of life, and she feels it is her duty to keep the checkbook balanced, be a good cook, and nurse her mate back to health when he's sick. Her house will be clean and cozy and she won't throw money away foolishly. She will also help her husband organize his life and be loyal and devoted to him. What else could he ask for?

The Gold Man

A woman who looks for the passion and excitement of a storybook romance would be better off looking for another type of man — try a Blue. Dreams of Romeo and Juliet might leave her filled with disappointment in a relationship with a Gold man.

Everything he does is practical and down to earth, including his love affairs. He may not show his love by serenading her under the stars, but he will be devoted to his wife and family. To a Gold man, his main duty and responsibility is to take care of his family by providing them with all their basic needs. He will make sure there is a roof over their heads and lots of food stored up for a rainy day.

Because marriage is one of the most important decisions in his life, the Gold man is particular about the woman he chooses. He will not be rushed into making his decision. He certainly doesn't want to make the wrong one. If she is patient and the right one for him, a woman can expect marriage to a Gold man to last until death does them part. Once he's made his decision, he isn't likely to change his mind.

His frugality probably will prevent him from showering her with excessive gifts, no matter how much money he has. But all of her basic necessities will be supplied, and he will be loyal and considerate. He will remember special dates and important things that matter to her. He will do what is necessary to keep a strong marriage together, but if she doesn't live up to being the partner he expects, watch out. He can be stubborn, and when he makes up his mind it's over, it's over. Sentimental memories are not enough to bring him back when he makes up his mind to move on.

A Gold man will expect his partner to dress smartly, not flashily. She should be more concerned about keeping him interested than attracting a lot of attention from others. More important than being sexy, she must be neat and clean. He is interested in a long-lasting and stable marriage with a wife, not a mistress.

He will not take his responsibility as a parent lightly. He is the type of father who makes sure the children do their homework, get involved with the right kinds of extracurricular activities, and go to good schools and colleges. Great emphasis is placed on education and good citizenship. Discipline is equally important, and he will probably not spoil his children. For a Gold man, to spare the rod is to spoil the child. He may be overly critical and will need to learn how to say "I love you" to his children.

For the woman who places a high value on security, he is the ideal man. He will be a hard-working husband who will provide for her and be a good father to his children. He will be well organized, remember their anniversaries, and seldom be interested in hanging out with the guys.

Gold Children

Gold children usually have a maturity level that exceeds their age, and from the time they are small, they tend to be neat and tidy. You can expect them to put their toys away without being told. They won't cause much trouble and will probably enjoy helping with the household chores.

Golds are obedient in school. The teacher will have no trouble disciplining them. They will learn early to do what they are supposed to do and to respect authority. Once they are told something is wrong, they will not have to be reminded. When I taught elementary school more than twenty years ago, the Gold kids did everything I told them and never got into trouble. Now I understand why.

Gold children can be rather modest and may not stand out in a crowd. They may feel inferior to the more popular and extroverted personalities who get most of the attention. Although they are probably self-sufficient, these children need your encouragement and it would be a mistake to assume they don't.

Like Blue children, Golds need lots of acknowledgment. Yet unlike Blues, who want to be acknowledged for who they are, Gold children need to be acknowledged for their accomplishments or achievements. Positive feedback reassures them that they are doing what they are "supposed to." Of course, it is also important to accept them for who they are, but because they are concrete thinkers, it is better to give examples of what you mean. For example, you might say to a Blue child, "I'm proud of you because you are so warm and kind." To a Gold child you would be more effective if you said, "I'm proud of you because you are doing so well in school and you always keep your room clean."

Gold children have their own internal schedule. They are most comfortable with a routine with which they can predict when to expect things to happen. Any change in their personal schedule can upset them. It is also better if they have their own rooms, because they are meticulous and fussy about having their belongings moved. They'll show a strong sense of responsibility early and will take good care of their belongings.

Make sure the rules are clear to them, because Golds need structure in their lives. They will not rebel against it; they actually feel secure when they know their boundaries. They want to obey you, but they must first know what is expected.

Gold Out-of-Esteem Behavior

Golds can become melancholy, pessimistic and inflexible when they are out-of-esteem. They can easily be disappointed by other people who don't live up to their standards of right and wrong behavior and what people "should" and "should not" do. Because they are self-disciplined, it is difficult for them to understand why everyone can't do what they are "supposed" to do. It is easy for Golds to get into black-or-white, either/or thinking with no room for individual needs or differences. They worry more than others, which can drive them to depression, especially when they cannot change others to live up to their standards. They may become pessimistic and critical of others. They may get into a rut that is difficult to escape. Many people say Golds have the ability to make others feel guilty and bad about themselves.

8

The Orange Personality
Where's the Action?

⟨ ⟨ ⟨ ⟨ ⟨ ⟨ ⟨ ⟨ ⟨ ⟨ ⟨ ⟩ ⟩ ⟩ ⟩ ⟩ ⟩ ⟩ ⟩ ⟩ ⟩ ⟩ ⟩

Without the magnificent, upbeat, light-hearted personality of the Orange, the rest of us would probably forget how to have fun. The most likely place to find an Orange is anywhere people are laughing and having a good time. Many get paid to entertain us. Typically, they are the ones at the center of attention. Most Oranges are extroverted characters with little modesty, although some are laid back and quiet. They number almost as many as the Golds, but there isn't much more the two colors have in common. Comedians like Joan Rivers, Eddie Murphy and Roseanne are examples of the extroverted Orange personality.

Oranges' attitude is "Live for today, for tomorrow is not promised." Consequently, it is difficult for them to save, store or prepare. What if tomorrow never comes? They live life in the present — what is happening right now is most important. They don't take life as seriously as other types, because they know life is supposed to be fun. Often their behavior can appear childlike — not childish, but full of spontaneity and action. In this sense they are real-life Peter Pans, who never want to grow up or grow old — the epitome of true free spirits who cannot be confined or tied down.

Oranges are fantastic movers and shakers who live life to the fullest with more action and energy than the rest of us can muster. Donald Trump, the flamboyant entrepreneur, has been described as possessing this quality. An interviewer from a popular magazine described his office as a "well-run vaudeville show." There were so many people walking in and out with different agendas, and so many phone calls during his interview, that it left the interviewer feeling dizzy. Only an Orange could feel comfortable and function in such a frenetic environment.

It is difficult to ignore the high energy level of the more extroverted Oranges. They have loud voices and are usually doing several things at one time. Those of us who are different may look at them and shake our heads in amazement that they can accomplish any task in the midst of what looks like utter confusion to the rest of us. Oranges say it is not distracting to have many things going on simultaneously. In fact, they wouldn't have it any other way. If you spend a lot of time with an Orange, get used to it.

They have a frankness of speech that can set many people off, but Oranges don't necessarily say things in malice. They will impulsively blurt things out without thinking how they might hurt another person. If they do hurt or offend unintentionally, they will be first to bring a gift to apologize for their rash behavior.

Oranges don't hang onto hurt or anger. They manage to get it out somehow, sometimes in the form of retaliation. They are the least likely to have ulcers, because they don't sit and wallow in their emotions.

Someone who is easily offended may find it difficult to be around Oranges. Though sometimes blunt in their speech, they can be surprised when people tell them that they hurt their feelings. They are blunt, not brutal. What is on their minds comes off their tongues. An Orange friend of mine looked at my car one day and commented on how dirty it was. As if that weren't enough, he went on to say that people who drive expensive cars like mine should take better care of them. My car *was* dirty, but his words still hurt my feelings!

Oranges are kind and generous to the people they care about. No one will buy you a more extravagant gift or give you a bigger party than an Orange. It is a good idea also to be generous when you give them gifts. They probably won't forget it when it's time to reciprocate.

Oranges move rapidly and don't stay in one place long. Sitting too long causes restlessness and boredom. They find it difficult to get through the day without taking a lot of breaks. They may need to take a walk every couple of hours to revitalize their energy in order to concentrate on work.

Traveling appeals to Oranges because they love the change in environment and the excitement of the unpredictable. Margaret looks forward to her frequent trips even if they're only for three-day weekends. Whether it's a scenic trip up the coast from Los Angeles to Santa Barbara or a one-hour plane ride to Las Vegas, she says, "I need to get away from my regular, daily routine and do something different." Often these trips are not planned and she has no idea what she will do when she arrives. "That's part of the excitement," she explains.

Plunging into love affairs is easy, but marriage is another story. Oranges can be exciting and romantic lovers who will wine and dine their partners. But unless they are ready to settle down, don't be surprised when they disappear. Feeling a certain way today doesn't mean they will feel the same tomorrow. Oranges who marry later in life stand a better chance of having a lasting relationship. Be prepared for the unexpected and you will never be surprised, but there is never a dull moment with an Orange.

Like Golds, Oranges are good at remembering details. They can tell someone what happened on a specific date, or every detail about a room or a movie, but they have a habit of forgetting more mundane things like their belongings. It is not uncommon for them to lose a lot of car and door keys, wallets, jackets and sunglasses.

Orange Goals and Ideals

The one thing Oranges love more than competition is winning. If you compete with them, be prepared to stick it out, because their goal is to win. They don't do things for deep meaning like Blues do, or to prove how smart they are like Greens. Oranges win for the sake of winning. The act of winning builds their self-esteem and confidence. Donald Trump expressed this attitude when he said, "We're here and we live our sixty, seventy or eighty years and we're gone. They win, you win, and in the end it doesn't mean a hell of a lot. But it is something to do — to keep you interested."

Oranges cannot tolerate boredom, which is the exact opposite of their mission to experience life to its fullest. When Donald Trump was asked how much is enough, he said, "As long as I enjoy what I'm doing without getting bored or tired...the sky's the limit." Action is the antidote to boredom. Do something — almost anything!

Like many Oranges, Matt Groening found a creative way to fight boredom in school. He said, "I got in trouble for drawing cartoons. They used to get confiscated. In fact, one of the great thrills of my life is that I now get paid for what I used to get sent to the principal's office for. I spent many long hours in the principal's office staring at the ceiling and counting the little dots in the tile." If you've watched Groening's TV series, *The Simpsons*, you know what Bart Simpson does when he gets bored in school.

To affect Oranges, things must be concrete and practical, never abstract. Appeal to one or more of their five senses — sight, sound, touch, taste or smell — to get their attention. Show them how they can use something. If you want to sell them on an idea, show them its practical use. You can't talk to Oranges in the same language that you use for Blues or Greens. Tell Blues how something will help others reach their potential; tell Greens that a particular idea will create positive change. When talking to Oranges, be more specific and practical, and use examples.

They can understand if you show them how to make money with an idea or how they can use it to make a particular thing happen. When they catch on, they will act and act quickly. I once told an Orange friend about an idea that I didn't plan to implement for six months. She immediately wanted to get off the phone and start working on it. When I told her I thought it was too soon, she said, "Why wait? In six months someone else will already have acted on our idea. We have to do it now."

Unlike Golds, Oranges hate to practice anything. Golds can sit and practice the piano or guitar until they learn to play a song. Oranges prefer to learn by performing. To them, time is better spent playing with a band or group and learning by doing. Just don't call it practice or rehearsal. Many Orange athletes perfect their sport on the schoolyard or wherever they can find a game. They will play for hours on end and develop great skill in the process. The outcome is the same as for someone who practices; they both perfect the activity. The difference is that Oranges actually play the sport, and have a good time, while improving their technique.

Physical activity is a must, judging by the number of Oranges who pursue competitive sports or make regular visits to the gym. Without physical activity, Oranges may feel like their energy is bottled up. When they feel upset or angry, they use physical activity to release these emotions.

Hollywood is filled with Orange personalities. Quick on their feet, they can be highly talented and creative. Oranges range from actors to comedians, stuntmen, musicians, singers, and dancers, all of whom thrive in an atmosphere of flexible schedules and freedom of expression.

Oranges like to take risks. Racetracks and casinos attract Oranges like nectar attracts bees. Of course, they are optimistic enough to think they will win. Donald Trump is certainly not afraid to take financial risks. He thinks it's fun to build a bigger building, buy a bigger boat or negotiate a bigger deal.

Oranges are also more likely than other types to take physical risks. Think of the race-car driver, the bungee jumper or the sky-diver. The rush that Oranges get from these activities makes the risk worthwhile. Although competitive sports may not be as dangerous, athletes risk bodily injuries each time they play a game. Their lack of fear allows them to take more risks and become the best at their sport.

Oranges take a light-hearted attitude toward life. Life is to be enjoyed at every opportunity. Others benefit from their playful nature and great sense of humor. They're the ones most likely to tell jokes and make the rest of us laugh. They remind us all not to take life too seriously. They certainly don't.

The Orange Woman

The Orange woman stands out in a crowd because she is a friendly, charming conversationalist who has the ability to talk to anyone easily. If she is an extrovert, she might be described as having the gift of gab. People are attracted to her as they are to Blue women, but for different reasons. A Blue woman is easy to talk to because she is an attentive listener who shows a lot of compassion for others. An Orange woman is light-hearted and a lot of fun to be with. She also dresses in a manner that attracts attention. Bold in her fashion, she is not intimidated by loud colors, sexy clothes, and trendy styles.

As a very independent woman, an Orange has a life of her own. With all her interests and hobbies, there is no time for boredom. Traveling is one of her favorite things to do — preferably first class. She is by nature extravagant and she loves to spend money. She loves good food and fine wine almost as much as she loves shopping for clothes. The man in her life needs to be loaded, because saving money is not in her cards. The trade-off for him is that she won't be a clinging vine — she is on the go too much to have time for that.

Playing a passive female role in a relationship is not her cup of tea. She is frank with men and says what she thinks. A man may at times be put off, but at least she will be honest and not play games. With an Orange woman, what you see is truly what you get. She has no respect for wishy-washy men, so he must be straightforward and honest.

Sometimes an Orange woman can be too trusting in her relationships with men, taking them at surface value and mistaking their true depth. Friendship can seem like love to her, and she may give her heart away too quickly. She may have many unfulfilling relationships. Luckily, she bounces back quickly without having her spirit crushed. She's not necessarily looking to settle down with one man. In fact, she can be rather skittish about marriage, because she is afraid of losing her freedom. But as with most women, if the right man comes along it's hard to resist.

It's not uncommon for her to be involved in show business. Many Orange women are drawn to the bright lights of Hollywood, as well as the Broadway stage. The sound of applause and the excitement of an audience are energizing. She needs a partner who will let her put her career first. If he gives her the freedom she needs, she will choose him when she's ready to settle down.

As a homemaker she is not conventional. She likes a clean house as much as anyone but doesn't want to be the one to clean it. The routine of putting the same dishes away over and over again and making the bed every day is a real drag. She may not be overjoyed about cooking, either, but at least she can be creative and provide lots of variety in her meals.

Because she collects friends everywhere she goes, she will probably have lots of company. She doesn't mind people stopping by unexpectedly. Unlike the Gold woman, it won't bother her if her house isn't perfect when guests come. Camaraderie is what is important, and she thrives on it. She doesn't mind setting extra places at the dinner table or bringing out the extra bed for guests to spend the night.

She will be more of a buddy to her children than other women because she knows how to play and have fun with them. They may think of her more as a big sister than a mother. There won't be many dull moments in an Orange woman's house.

The Orange Man

If a woman is looking for a romantic relationship that is full of fun and excitement, Mr. Orange could be the man for her. On the other hand, if she needs the security of knowing that he will always be there for her, he could cause her to feel insecure. He may call her one day to play at the beach, ride bikes, go to dinner and dance the night away. She may be impressed when he showers her with all kinds of gifts, flowers and perfume. Her time with him will be happy and cheerful as she laughs at his clever jokes and appreciates his light-hearted attitude about life. He might even say "I love you," and convince her that she has found true love.

The next time she hears from him may be a week or a month later, which can leave her baffled and depressed about his unpredictability. But it's his nature to be unpredictable. The next time he calls, he may be surprised at her cold, distant attitude. Didn't the two of them have a romantic, exciting time together the last time he saw her? What about all the times he said "I love you"? He meant everything he said at the time, but he didn't necessarily mean that he would love her forever, or even next week. If she is an incurable romantic and needs consistency, harmony and perfect love in her life, she could be in for a life of disappointment and trouble with an Orange man.

Freedom is a must for the Orange man. Quick to get involved in relationships, he is as quick to get uninvolved. If he's not ready to settle down, long, drawn-out courtships can be unappealing to him, and deep emotional commitments can make him feel trapped. Others need to understand that he lives so much in the present that what is right for him now may be a lie tomorrow. If he feels pressured, he may resolve the problem by disappearing, off to find another place and other people to be with who are more light-hearted about life.

An eternal optimist, he never stops to worry about what happened yesterday or what could happen tomorrow. He may rush into financial matters as he does relationships, with blind faith that things will work out in a positive way. He doesn't usually stop to analyze people or situations long enough to avoid embarrassing moments. He may be too trusting of other people. Either he is lucky, or when his luck runs out he recovers quickly. Life is to be enjoyed, and somehow things always get better.

For a partner who likes to have fun, this relationship could work out. The Orange man likes variety and stimulation, so a woman must be prepared to be busy. It helps if she likes sports, because more than likely he will. He may want to take her along to all his social activities with his buddies. She should also expect to do a lot of traveling with him, but it's a good idea for her to have plenty of interests of her own to keep her busy when he's not around.

As a father, he will probably treat his kids more like pals. He won't be strict, and he will allow them more autonomy than most fathers. Playing with the boys may be more comfortable than playing with the girls, unless they have a thick skin. Because he enjoys the outdoors, camping, amusement parks and the zoo can be appealing places to go. Like his children, he knows how to have a good time. His bluntness may be too harsh for more sensitive kids, but he will usually compensate with his good sense of humor.

Orange Children

With Orange children, you have your work cut out for you. They are active by nature and need a lot of space in which to move around. These are not the type of children to confine to a playpen like their Gold, Green or Blue counterparts. They will probably walk and talk early and get into everything. The more introverted Orange children will not be as active, but they may seem active compared to other children. Have a variety of toys for them and lots of pictures, books and bright colors to stimulate them. They love to do several things at once and their quick movements may make you nervous, but you'd better get used to it. They are adventurous, so forget about keeping them clean. You can't change their basic nature any more than you can change the stripes on a tiger.

Orange children will be happy, playful bundles of energy, the kind you may think will never grow up. To some extent they will maintain their childlike nature, unless it is squelched. You may ask yourself why they run around so much or why they get into one thing after another. They're being themselves. They may be awkward and clumsy — spilling at the table and falling down and hurting themselves. Orange girls may be tomboys and prefer not to wear dresses.

You can't easily control Orange children. They can be defiant and rebel against too much structure. They get into trouble with authority figures, since they won't obey rules just because they are supposed to, as Gold kids will. Teachers may have a difficult time with them. Orange kids have a low tolerance for too many strict rules and regulations. They are more apt to buy into rules concerned with their well-being than rules based on established social mores.

Their restlessness and boredom are likely to show up in school. If learning is too dull, boring and routine, they are likely to get into trouble with their teacher. They will sometimes get up and walk around when they are not supposed to because sitting for long periods of time is difficult for them. School authorities often label these kids hyperactive and suggest medication. Is something wrong with these kids, or is it the school system's outdated, unimaginative teaching methods? The Orange learning style is interactive and hands-on. Traditional schools can actually stifle learning in Orange kids, who are the ones most likely to drop out.

Orange children are competitive and they like to win. Also, they are not afraid of a good fight and they can push others to the limit without compromising. And since they do not like losing, they need to be taught how to be good sports when this happens.

Don't expect them to be neat and tidy like Gold kids. Their rooms are likely to be in a constant state of disarray, with clothes and toys all over the place, so they will probably need some help on how to be organized. You can be firm about your expectations from them, but the thing to remember is that you will never turn these kids into Gold children.

Orange Out-of-Esteem Behavior

We are always striving to obtain self-esteem, and our inner values determine how we seek to acquire this esteem. Oranges' need for spontaneity, action, freedom and excitement can lead them to self-destructive behavior when they are out-of-esteem. When they don't feel good about themselves, it deprives them of their ability to enjoy life in the moment — their favorite place to be. The quick fix of outside stimulants, such as drugs and alcohol, seems appealing when they want to feel uplifted. Stimulants give a false sense of well-being that can easily become addictive. Other addictions can include sex, gambling, overeating, ciga- rettes, and caffeine. Oranges must be careful to have their needs met in positive ways to avoid the risks inherent in immediate gratification.

The need for stimulation can get Oranges into situations they may later regret, but which seem to be the only answer at the time. They may push their luck to the limit and not back away from a fight. Some Oranges have violent tempers, and if you start a fight with them, be prepared to finish it. Their style is not to run away or try to talk someone out of a confrontation. Oranges may speak or act first and think of the consequences later. They can be stubborn and determined to have things their way. If someone does something to harm them, they are known to retaliate. An Orange extrovert is more likely to strike back, but an introvert could repress violent thoughts until they overflow into action.

Oranges must find positive ways to channel their energy. Exercise is one example: many Oranges say they get depressed without it.

When Oranges are in esteem they can make things happen quickly, but when out-of-esteem they can procrastinate. They may not complete things they start, or avoid things they need to do to be successful in their personal or professional lives. Often they have good intentions to get things done but get sidetracked by other things and never find the time. It must have been an Orange who first said, "Out of sight, out of mind."

9

Four Paths to a Successful Life's Work

‹ ‹ ‹ ‹ ‹ ‹ ‹ ‹ ‹ ‹ ‹ ‹ › › › › › › › › › › › ›

A musician must make music, an artist must paint,
a poet must write, if he is to be ultimately at peace
with himself. What a man can do, he must do. He must
be true to his own nature.

Abraham Maslow

Your life's work allows you to express your true nature. Most of us were not told that everything we need to do work that makes us happy and successful is already within us. I believe we are all here to make a contribution to society in our own unique ways, and when we use our personality strengths and talents to do our work, we are being true to our own nature.

Because we are continually striving to meet our needs, a job description won't prevent us from trying to do what we naturally love. Frustration sets in, however, when our job duties run counter to our internal motivation. Often we will attempt to bend job descriptions to fit what we enjoy doing. Several years ago, I worked with a woman in a college career center who tried to bend her job to fit.

Louise and Joan were hired to do similar clerical jobs. Their duties included answering the phone, making appointments, administering tests, and assisting people in finding occupational information. Joan was consistent about doing her work according to her job description. Louise, however, was repeatedly reprimanded for not doing what she was hired to do.

These women had differing personality traits. Joan, a Gold woman in her forties, was not shy but certainly not an extrovert either. After getting her college degree she had focused her attention on raising two sons and worked part-time to help support the family. Although she was overqualified for the job in the career center, Joan wanted it because it fit well around her family schedule. She enjoyed organizing the center. Everyone acknowledged her for being a efficient worker who could always be counted on to get the job done in a timely manner.

Louise was a bubbly, friendly and extremely gregarious Blue personality. She was the one person in the center who everyone knew, because she made it a point to talk to anyone who walked in. So many students dropped in to see her on a regular basis that it was almost as though she had a following. Sometimes she would spend hours talking to the same person.

As the coordinator of the career center, it was called to my attention that Louise's clerical duties were going undone while she spent a tremendous amount of time "counseling." This created a serious problem because, at the time, she was not qualified to be a counselor.

I encouraged Louise to continue her education so that she could someday become a counselor, because she did it so naturally and it was obviously what she really wanted to do. She took my advice and transferred to a university to pursue a counseling degree.

Notice that although both women were hired to do the same job, they expressed themselves uniquely in the role. Each focused on activities that she naturally enjoyed doing.

I've observed that people are much happier when what they are paid to do is consistent with who they are. Some of you will feel a need to make your contribution on a grand scale while others will not. It is not the size of your contribution that counts; what makes the difference is how much you enjoy what you do. Gloria Steinem and Martin Luther King, Jr., needed to impact social and political systems to make their contribution to other people's lives. I know a woman who above everything else prefers to be a secretary. She feels good about her ability to organize her boss's life and she has no desire to be the boss. If what you are doing makes you happy, stick with it.

As Maslow said, finding the work that you are "fitted to do" is the key to doing what you love. Some people, like Mother Teresa, refer to their life's work as their destiny. Others say their life's work is something they would do even if they weren't paid. Some say they can remember doing their work before they were ever paid for it. A sister of mine, who is a hairdresser today, grew up playing with everybody's hair and the hair on her dolls. She knew she would someday become a hairdresser because she always loved styling hair.

I can remember my friends coming to me to tell me their problems long before I became a counselor. They said I always made them feel better. What they didn't know was that I got as much benefit from helping them as they did from being helped. I was doing my life's work without knowing it. I enjoyed what I was doing and my self-esteem soared. Helping others makes me feel good about myself.

The following section will help you discover your true values, natural gifts and talents, and will offer suggestions for your life's work.

Job titles are not important. What matters is whether the work represents what is important to you (your values), and what you spend your time doing (skills used). The occupations listed for each color barely scratch the surface of all the possibilities open to you, but the awareness of your true values, natural gifts and talents provides information needed to decide if a particular career is a match for you.

Once you are clear about what you need in your work for it to be enjoyable, the *Dictionary of Occupational Titles* (DOT) and the *Occupational Outlook Handbook* (OOH) — two major publications from the U.S. Department of Labor — will be very useful in researching other options.

The DOT lists over 35,000 job titles and the OOH includes more specific information such as job descriptions, educational requirements, training, salary ranges, and places of employment. Both publications can be found in libraries, and college and high school career centers. A new computer program, Occupational Information Network (ONET), will soon replace both these publications.

My suggestions will get you started in the right direction. Once you have completed this process of self-discovery, you will be prepared to take advantage of the many available job search tools to find your own unique life's work. The first essential step, however, is to get a grip on who you are.

Read the appropriate section for your primary color and complete the exercises. Reread the information as often as you need.

If you have already identified your true self and have found your life's work, use these exercises to look for natural ways to extend and expand what you love to do. True Colors powerfully opened my eyes to becoming a writer — a natural extension of my life's work.

The Blue Path

Your need to make a difference in the lives of others is a big clue to the kind of work you can feel passionate about and that will bring a sense of fulfillment. You have great people skills and the ability to bring out the best in others. When you help others improve their lives it gives you the satisfaction of making the world a better place. More than for any other type, raising other people's self-esteem and encouraging them to reach their own potential come naturally to you. Because this comes from your heart, you are not always aware of what you do for others, but this gift is your way of making a contribution to the world.

Your communication skills play an important role in your ability to help others. Many Blues have used their talent as authors, counselors, motivational speakers and songwriters. Whatever outlet you choose, remember that your greatest strengths are your ability to communicate well and help others improve their lives.

If you spend the majority of your time working with data, like an accountant, or programming a computer, you will most likely feel like something is missing in your work. Work for you needs to have a higher calling than simply earning a paycheck. It must have meaning and purpose.

Blue True Values

The earlier chapter on the Blue personality discussed at length the true values that motivate and drive your behavior. The following list summarizes those values:

Authenticity
Being acknowledged
Communication
Compassion
Creativity
Democracy
Emotions
Empathy
Enthusiasm
Friendship
Harmony
Honesty
Individuality
Integrity
Intuition

Love
Natural potential
Optimism
Patience
Peace
Pleasing others
Positive feedback
Public contact
Relationships
Romance
Self-understanding
Sensitivity
Sincerity
Spirituality
Tact
Teamwork
Trustworthiness
Unity

Blue Natural Gifts and Talents

Your natural gifts are things that you are good at and enjoy doing. Notice how many of these skills involve helping other people, yet they are not specific to only one type of work. These are your transferable skills, which can be used in many diverse occupations. These skills will help you identify work that will give you a sense of passion and fulfillment. Put a star next to the skills you most prefer to use.

Acknowledging others — recognizing and validating others for who they are
Building rapport — bringing harmony to a relationship
Building self-esteem — helping others feel good about themselves
Communicating — effectively exchanging verbal or written information with others

Consulting — giving professional advice

Coordinating — bringing people and activities together in a harmonious way

Counseling — helping others with their personal and professional problems

Enlightening — giving spiritual insight

Expressing feelings — openly communicating feelings to other people

Facilitating groups — assisting a group to move harmoniously in a positive direction

Fostering — nurturing

Guiding others — steering or directing people in a positive direction

Healing — restoring to health

Helping others — improving the lives of others

Influencing others — having an effect on the lives of other people

Inspiring others — having an exalting influence upon others

Interviewing others — using good communication skills to obtain information from another person

Leading — acting as a positive role model more than being in a position of power or authority

Listening — hearing and paying attention to what others have to say

Mentoring — coaching and supporting others in the direction they want to go in

Motivating — acting as a catalyst to move others to action

Nurturing — developing and fostering the potential in others

Public speaking — effectively using language to make speeches in public

Recruiting — getting others involved in whatever they believe in

Supporting others — assisting others emotionally

Teaching — enlightening others and motivating them to learn

Training — directing the growth of others

Visualizing — imagining possibilities
Working as a team — bringing a group together to meet a
    common goal

Career Choices Suited for Blues

The following are examples of work suited for your true values and natural gifts and talents. Put a star next to the occupations that you would like to research for more information. You will want to know such things as the job duties, salary, education and training required, and where to look for this kind of work. Self-employment is also an option. Use these suggestions as a catalyst for your own thinking. Remember, thousands of other possibilities exist. Your local library or a career center will have resources to provide the information you need. I recommend talking to someone who is already doing the work you're interested in. Such a person can provide valuable firsthand information not otherwise available.

Actor
Aerobics Teacher
Airline Receptionist
Art Therapist
Career Coach
Career Counselor
Community Affairs Coordinator
Drug and Alcohol Counselor
Educational Consultant
Elementary School Teacher
Employment Interviewer
English Teacher
Family Child Care Provider
Family Lawyer
Fashion Designer

Fashion Editor
Fashion Writer
Flight Attendant
Foreign Language Interpreter
Foreign Language Teacher
Foreign Language Translator
Fundraiser
Greeting Card Writer
Gynecologist
Home Schooling Consultant
Home Tutor
Human Services Worker
Hypnotherapist
In-Home Health Care Provider
Journalist
Lawyer for Battered Women
Marketing Communication Expert
Marriage and Family Counselor
Metaphysical Teacher
Minister/Rabbi
Motivational Speaker
Music Teacher
News Reporter
Newscaster
Nun
Nutrition and Weight Loss Instructor
Pastoral Counselor
Pediatrician
Personal Coach
Poet
Psychiatric Social Worker
Psychic Reader
Psychology Teacher
Public Relations Specialist
Recreation Leader
Rehabilitation Counselor

School Counselor
Sign Language Interpreter
Singer
Skin Care Specialist
Social Science Teacher
Social Scientist
Social Worker
Speech Coach
Spiritual Counselor
Talk Show Host/Hostess
Team Building Consultant
Tour Guide
Training Specialist
Travel Agent
Wardrobe Consultant
Wedding Consultant
Writer of Children's Books
Writer of Non-Fiction Books
Writer of Romance Books

Now turn to the section, *Tying It All Together,* for more help in discovering your ultimate career — your life's work.

The Green Path

You have a passion for knowledge. Your ability to be a great thinker is your clue to finding your ideal work for making your contribution to the world. Like inventors and scientists, you are a problem-solver who comes up with great ideas. With a mind that never quits, you dream up new things that other people don't think of, always analyzing and trying to figure things out. It is important for you to take time to conceptualize; some of your best insights come to you during your "think" times.

So-called daydreaming gave a college student of mine a clue to his life's work. He was obese and bored and spent much of his time at home watching soap operas. As the TV droned on he would design buildings and draw the plans for them. He had been doing this since childhood but never thought of it as a clue to his ideal work. He gave some drawings and plans to friends who were architects and they started selling them to make money. It finally dawned on him that he could earn this money himself if he became an architect. He changed his major in school from psychology to architecture to pursue his dream.

Your great intuition and creativity give you the ability to visualize the future. Whether you are drawn to engineering, politics, or philosophy you will find a way to use your knowledge to make important changes in the world. There will be those who will not understand your need to be a change agent, but the world needs people like you; otherwise, there would never be any progress or growth. You will make your best contribution by following your natural inclination to improve systems. Let your vision and your innovative ideas be your guide to success.

Green True Values

The earlier chapter on the Green personality discussed at length the true values that motivate and drive your behavior. The following list summarizes those values:

Abstraction
Autonomy
Brevity
Cleverness
Competence
Cool-headed under pressure
Creativity
Curiosity
Ethics
Fairness
Focus
Future orientation
Ideas

Imagination
Independence
Ingenuity
Invention
Innovation
Intelligence
Knowledge
Logic
Mental challenge
Objectivity
Precise language
Privacy
Power
Rationality
Self-confidence
Theory
Truth
Vision
Wisdom

Green Natural Gifts and Talents

Your natural gifts are things that you are good at and enjoy doing. Notice the emphasis on mental activity, but these skills are not specific to only one type of work. These are your transferable skills, which can be used in many diverse occupations. These skills will help you identify work that will give you a sense of passion and fulfillment. Put a star next to the skills you most prefer to use.

Analyzing — separating or distinguishing the component parts of something so as to discover its true nature or inner relationships
Conceptualizing — forming abstract ideas in the mind
Consulting — giving technical information or providing ideas to define, clarify or sharpen procedures, capabilities or product

specifications

Critiquing — analyzing, evaluating or appreciating works of art

Curing — restoring to health after a disease

Debating — discussing a question by considering opposing arguments

Designing — mentally conceiving and planning

Developing — making something available to improve a situation

Diagnosing — analyzing the cause or nature of a condition, situation or problem

Editing — improving and directing publications

Generating ideas — brainstorming or dreaming up ideas

Intellectualizing — using the intellect rather than emotion or experience

Interpreting ideas — explaining the meaning of ideas

Inventing — developing or creating something for the first time

Learning — gaining knowledge

Observing — examining people, data or things scientifically

Problem solving — identifying key issues or factors in a problem, generating ideas and solutions to solve the problem, selecting the best approach, and testing and evaluating it

Proofreading — reading and marking corrections

Reasoning — thinking

Researching — investigating and experimenting aimed at the discovery and interpretation of facts

Synthesizing — integrating ideas and information

Thinking logically — subjecting ideas to the process of logical thought

Writing — expressing by means of words

Career Choices Suited for Greens

The following are examples of work suited for your true values and natural gifts and talents. Put a star next to the occupations that you would like to research for more information. You will want to know such things as the job duties, salary, education and training required, and where to look for this kind of work. Self-employment is also an option. Use these suggestions as a catalyst for your own thinking. Remember, thousands of other possibilities exist. Your local library or a career center will have resources to provide the information you need. I recommend talking to someone who is already doing the work you're interested in. Such a person can provide valuable firsthand information not otherwise available.

Actor
Acupuncturist
Advertising Executive
Airplane Pilot
Anthropologist
Archaeologist
Architect
Art Advisor
Art Critic
Artist
Astronomer
Astrophysicist
Biomedical Engineer
Biomedical Researcher
Book Publisher
Chemist
College Professor/Researcher
Columnist
Computer Consultant
Computer Scientist
Computer Systems Analyst
Consultant
Criminal Lawyer
Criminologist
Dairy Scientist
Debater

Dentist
Ecologist
Editor
Engineer
FBI Agent
Geophysicist
Ghost Writer
Grant Writer
Graphic Artist
Industrial Designer
Inventor
Journalist
Lyricist
Marine Biologist
Math Teacher
Medical Doctor
Medical Researcher
Motion Picture Director
Motion Picture Producer
Movie Critic
News Writer
Newspaper Editor
Nuclear Medicine Technologist
Oceanographer
On-Line Multimedia Content Developer
Operations and Systems Researcher
Photographer
Physician's Assistant
Playwright
Podiatrist
Psychiatrist
Psychologist
Radiologist
Science Teacher
Scriptwriter

Software Programmer
Speech Pathologist
Speech Writer
Stockbroker
Surgeon
Technical Writer
Textbook Writer
TV News Broadcaster
Veterinarian
Writer of Science Fiction Books

Now turn to the section, *Tying It All Together*, for more help in discovering your ultimate career — your life's work.

The Gold Path

You desire to be responsible and do your duty. You are the maintainers of society, and without your ability to organize and implement what others create, there would be no stability in the world. Someone has to keep things running smoothly, and no one does it better than you. You are self-motivated and know how to discipline yourself to do what is expected of you.

You want to contribute by serving others, but in a way that is different from how a Blue wants to serve others. Whereas a Blue enjoys serving by encouraging others to reach their own potential, you want to help others be responsible and carry their load in the world. It is important to you that all do their share rather than depend on others to take care of them. Whether you are a teacher, supervisor, or school librarian, you will use your position to teach others to be more responsible.

Your belief in following the rules leads you to roles requiring you to see that others do the same. You are attracted to roles such as judge, school principal or police officer.

Many Golds also enjoy serving by taking care of other people's needs. Unlike Blues, who focus on the emotional needs of others, as a Gold you prefer to meet physical needs. You may be the nurse that takes care of patients, the manager who looks after everyone's schedules, or the administrative assistant who takes care of the boss's needs.

Let your ability to be well organized, detail oriented, and self disciplined guide you toward your life's work.

Gold True Values

The earlier chapter on the Gold personality discussed at length the true values that motivate and drive your behavior. The following list summarizes those values:

Accuracy
Achievement
Affiliation
Authority
Being meticulous
Caution
Community
Compensation
Completion
Conformity
Cooperation
Decisiveness
Dependability
Duty
Efficiency
Facts and data
Family
Justice
Loyalty
Morality
Orderliness
Predictability
Prestige

Profit
Punctuality
Recognition
Religion
Respect
Responsibility
Routine
Rules
Safety
Security
Service
Stability
Status
Structure
Tradition
Wealth

Gold Natural Gifts and Talents

Your natural gifts are things that you are good at and enjoy doing. Notice the emphasis on implementation, but these skills are not specific to only one type of work. These are your transferable skills, which can be used in many diverse occupations. These skills will help you identify work that will give you a sense of passion and fulfillment. Put a star next to the skills you most prefer to use.

Administering policies — managing a course or method of action
Allocating resources — designating resources for a specific purpose
Attending to detail — paying attention to small items
Bookkeeping — recording the accounts or transactions of a business
Budgeting — planning the amount of money that is available for, required for, or assigned to a particular purpose

Calculating — determining by mathematical means

Caretaking — taking care of the physical needs of others, especially children, the sick and the elderly

Collecting data — gathering information

Coordinating — taking care of logistics for events to flow smoothly

Decision-making — bringing things to a conclusion

Delegating — entrusting responsibilities to other people

Dispatching — sending off or away with promptness

Establishing procedures — constructing a series of steps to be followed in accomplishing something

Estimating cost — judging approximately the value or worth of something

Evaluating — appraising the worth, significance or status of something

Following directions — doing specifically the things told to do by others verbally or in writing

Following through — completing an activity planned or begun

Guarding — protecting or defending

Maintaining schedules — overseeing something designated for a fixed, future time

Maintaining records — accurate and up-to-date record keeping

Managing — directing or conducting business or affairs

Monitoring — watching, observing or checking for a specific purpose

Organizing — arranging things in a systematic order

Paying attention to detail — looking for smaller elements

Planning — making a way of proceeding

Preparing — getting something ready for use or getting ready for some occasion

Recording — putting things in writing

Regulating — governing or directing according to rule or law

Securing — Relieving from exposure to danger

Serving — making a contribution to the welfare of others

Supervising — Taking responsibility for the work done by others

Career Choices Suited for Golds

The following are examples of work suited for your true values and natural gifts and talents. Put a star next to the occupations that you would like to research for more information. You will want to know such things as the job duties, salary, education and training required, and where to look for this kind of work. Self-employment is also an option. Use these suggestions as a catalyst for your own thinking. Remember, thousands of other possibilities exist. Your local library or a career center will have resources to provide the information you need. I recommend talking to someone who is already doing the work you're interested in. Such a person can provide valuable firsthand information not otherwise available.

Accountant
Administrative Assistant
Air Traffic Controller
Archivist and Curator
Auditor
Bank Officer
Bank Teller
Bookkeeper
Budget Analyst
Business Teacher
Cashier
Claims Clerk
Closet Organizer
Collection Agent
Computer Programmer
Computer Security Specialist
Corporate Lawyer
Corrections Officer
Court Reporter
Data Entry Operator
Dental Hygienist

Dentist
Economist
Elementary School Teacher
Financial Planner
Food Service Manager
Forester
Geneticist
Geriatric Care Manager
History Teacher
Hospital Administrator
Hotel and Restaurant Manager
Human Resource Manager
Insurance Agent
Judge
Legal Assistant
Librarian
Loan Officer
Math Teacher
Medical Billing Service
Medical Doctor
Nun
Nurse
Occupational Therapist
Paralegal/Legal Assistant
Payroll Clerk
Pharmacist
Physical Therapist
Police Officer
Politician
Post Office Clerk
Public Administrator
Radiology Technician
Real Estate Agent or Broker
Receptionist
Recreational Therapist
Reservation Manager

Reunion Planner
School Administrator
School Counselor
Special Events Planner
Statistical Clerk
Statistician
Telephone Operator
Urban Planner

Now turn to the section, *Tying It All Together*, for more help in discovering your ultimate career — your life's work.

The Orange Path

You need action and excitement in your work. You are the most free-spirited of all colors, and you are at your best when you are left alone to do things your own way and at your own pace without too much structure. You like to do things quickly and you get bored if you spend too much time doing the same thing. The minute something becomes routine you become restless and lose interest. You are not going to spend a lot of time thinking about things like the Greens. Nor will you spend a lot of time organizing things like the Golds. You prefer to figure things out as you do them and you have a strong need to be doing something most of the time.

Having the freedom to experience life at every moment is the best way for you to make your contribution. You must act now — not later. Waiting is psychological death to you and certainly not the best use of your energy. Greens and Blues want to make changes and Golds want to maintain status quo. You are not concerned about either of these goals, which is why you are attracted to work where action is required. Nothing could be worse than asking you to sit behind a desk eight hours a day. Some of you will find your life's work as salespeople, entrepreneurs, bartenders, models, hairdressers, waitresses, race-car drivers or athletes.

Many of you have a physical ability to make your contribution to the world. You are the people who like to use your hands to make things that provide a more pleasant life for us all. Who better to build our buildings and cities?

Variety is essential in your work. To do the same thing over and over again all day long would be sheer boredom. Some people get confused by having too much variety in their work, but not you. The more variety, the more interesting the work is to you. I met a telephone operator who was bored with sitting and answering the phone all day. She was anxious to find other work. When she discovered she was Orange, she immediately went to her personnel office and asked about sales work for the company. She was promoted and found her niche.

A man I know who works for a rental car service is excited about the variety in his work. He loves the job because he does so many different things. He answers the phone, helps customers at the desk, takes them to their rental cars, and sometimes drives them to their own cars upon return. He also loves the opportunity to work a day in the field, one day a week, visiting different accounts. Only an Orange would be excited about work that contains so much action and variety.

Your spontaneity, high energy, and risk-taking ability are also clues to finding your life's work.

Orange True Values

The earlier chapter on the Orange personality discussed at length the true values that motivate and drive your behavior. The following list summarizes those values:

Action and activity
Adventure
Aesthetics
Artistic creativity
Camaraderie
Change

Competition
Energy
Entertainment
Excitement
Fast pace
Flexibility
Freedom
Fun
Generosity
Humor
Independence
Optimism
Physical challenge
Playfulness
Pleasure
Profit
Skillfulness
Spontaneity
Variety

Orange Natural Gifts and Talents

Your natural gifts are things that you are good at and enjoy doing. Notice the emphasis on activity, but these skills are not specific to only one type of work. These are your transferable skills, which can be used in many diverse occupations. These skills will help you identify work that will give you a sense of passion and fulfillment. Put a star next to the skills you most prefer to use.

Assembling things — fitting together the parts of things
Coaching — training intensively by instruction, demonstration and practice
Competing — challenging another for the purpose of winning
Constructing — building something
Dancing — performing rhythmic and patterned bodily movements, usually to music

Displaying things — arranging something in an eye-catching exhibit

Drafting — drawing the preliminary sketch, version or plan for something

Entertaining — performing publicly for amusement

Farming — engaging in raising crops or livestock

Gardening — cultivating a plot of ground with herbs, fruits, flowers or vegetables

Illustrating — providing with visual features intended to explain or decorate

Influencing others — causing an effect on others

Manipulating — treating or operating with the hands or by mechanical means

Manufacturing — making from raw materials by hand or by machinery

Marketing — planning and strategizing how to present a product or service in the marketplace

Negotiating — conferring with another so as to arrive at the settlement of some matter

Operating tools — skillfully handling tools to perform work

Operating vehicles — driving cabs, limousines, heavy equipment and so on

Performing — practicing an art that involves public performance

Persuading — influencing others in favor of a product, service, or point of view

Promoting — persuading people to see the value of an idea, person, activity or cause

Public Speaking — expressing yourself before a group

Repairing — restoring by replacing a part or putting together what is torn or broken

Responding to emergencies — being spontaneous and level-headed in emergency situations

Risk-taking — having a dangerous element to life

Selling — promoting a service or product with the intent of getting someone to buy or accept it in exchange for something, usually money

Troubleshooting — resolving disputes or obstructions
Working under pressure — working in situations where time
     pressure is prevalent

Career Choices Suited for Oranges

The following are examples of work suited for your true values and natural gifts and talents. Put a star next to the occupations that you would like to research for more information. You will want to know such things as the job duties, salary, education and training required, and where to look for this kind of work. Self-employment is also an option. Use these suggestions as a catalyst for your own thinking. Remember, thousands of other possibilities exist. Your local library or a career center will have resources to provide the information you need. I recommend talking to someone who is already doing the work you're interested in. Such a person can provide valuable firsthand information not otherwise available.

Acting Coach
Actor
Advertising Sales Representative
Athletic Coach
Auto Mechanic
Bartender
Broadcast Technician
Carpenter
Cartoonist
Chef
Child Care Worker
Chiropractor
Choreographer
Clown
Comedian
Commercial Artist
Computer Operator

Computer Service Technician
Cosmetologist
Cruise Director
Dance Teacher
Dancer
Disc Jockey
Electronics Technician
Event Creation Coordinator
Fashion Illustrator
Fashion Model
Firefighter
Flight Attendant
Graphic Design Artist
Helicopter Pilot
Illustrator
Independent Video Producer
Industrial Arts Teacher
Interior Designer
Jewelry Maker
Jockey
Labor Relations Specialist
Lifeguard
Lobbyist
Magician
Marketing Specialist
Mechanical Engineer
Media Relations Executive
Mediator
Mime
Motion Picture Producer
Musician
Painter
Paramedic
Park Ranger
Party Planner
Photojournalist

Physical Education Teacher
Physical Therapist
Plumber
Police Officer
Politician
Professional Athlete
Property Manager
Public Relations Specialist
Public Speaker
Puppeteer
Race-Car Driver
Radio or TV Announcer
Real Estate Agent
Restaurant Consultant
Sales Representative
Sculptor
Secret Service Agent
Set Designer
Sound Technician
Sports Nutritionist
Travel Consultant
Trial Lawyer
Truck Driver
Voice-Over Artist
Waiter or Waitress
X-ray Technician

Now you are ready for the next section, *Tying It All Together*, for more help in discovering your ultimate career — your life's work.

Tying It All Together

Now that you are more knowledgeable about your values, talents, and possible career choices, it is time to use this information to make a decision about the direction you want to take in your work. This process can become clearer if you begin by determining what your purpose is in life. The exercise on the next page will assist you in writing a life mission statement to bring clarity to your purpose.

Your Life Mission Statement

It is important to create a life mission statement. Writing a statement about your own personal mission will help you get clearer about the direction you want your life's work to take. Successful companies write a mission statement for an important reason: to explicitly state the purpose of the company and what they want to achieve. A mission statement provides needed direction and makes it clear when they are meeting their intentions and when they are not. When they are off course, the mission statement is their guide to what is needed to get back in alignment with their mission.

To stay on track, you need a mission statement to direct your life's work. This is not a specific statement about the work you do. Rather, it describes how you want to make your contribution to society. While it is more of a general statement of what your life is about — the things you value and want to be remembered for — it also includes your natural gifts, talents, strengths, skills, and passions.

What is the legacy you want to leave behind? The work you love is an important way to express your life's mission. For example, here is my life mission statement: My mission is to motivate, inspire, and guide the natural potential in myself and others.

Now you are ready to take steps to create your own life mission statement.

Writing Your Life Mission Statement

Step One

Choose three verbs from the natural gifts and talents list for your primary color that identify what you want to do.

1. I want to _____

2. I want to _____

3. I want to _____

Step Two

Choose a major value of yours, something that drives you, from the list of true values for your primary color.

A major value of mine is _____

Step Three

Choose the population you want to serve (a particular age group, race, gender, or special population, such as the homeless, the physically challenged, pregnant teenagers).

I want to serve

_____

Now you are ready to write your own life mission statement.

My mission is to _____

_____

_____

The diagram below shows how to summarize your life's work which is at the center of your true values, natural gifts and talents and the career choices you are best suited for.

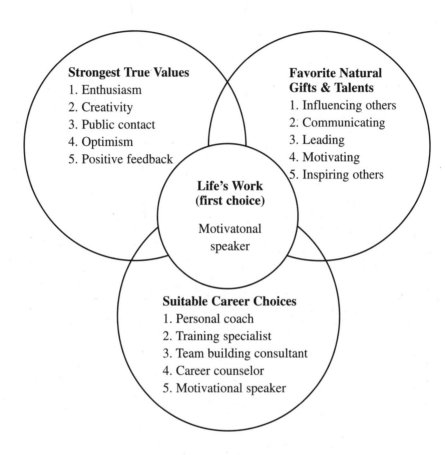

Strongest True Values
1. Enthusiasm
2. Creativity
3. Public contact
4. Optimism
5. Positive feedback

Favorite Natural Gifts & Talents
1. Influencing others
2. Communicating
3. Leading
4. Motivating
5. Inspiring others

Life's Work (first choice)

Motivatonal speaker

Suitable Career Choices
1. Personal coach
2. Training specialist
3. Team building consultant
4. Career counselor
5. Motivational speaker

Example

It is time to put the information in this chapter together. You need to answer the same questions as Michelle did in Chapter 3: What motivates you and what do you enjoy doing? List five of your strongest true values in the circle on the top left of the following diagram. Next list five of your favorite natural gifts and talents in the top right circle. Choose five careers from your primary color group or any other resource that will allow you to express your values and utilize your best gifts and talents. Your life's work is the best choice — your ultimate career — at the center of your true values, natural gifts and talent and the career choices you are best suited for. How much time it takes you depends on where you are now. It is most important to begin to take steps moving you in the direction that takes you forward in your life.

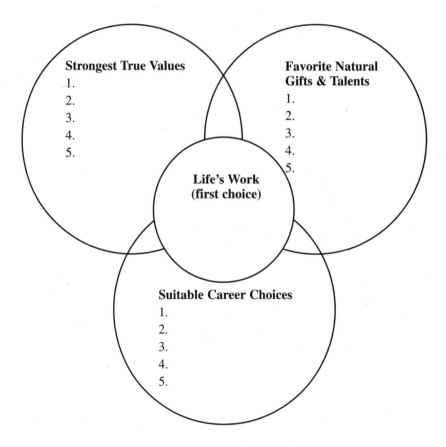

The following chapters will help you figure out the blocks to your success and how to eliminate them in order to create your ideal life's work.

10

Dream Buster — Facing Fear

‹ ‹ ‹ ‹ ‹ ‹ ‹ ‹ ‹ ‹ ‹ › › › › › › › › › › › ›

Feel the Fear and Do it Anyway
Title of a book by Susan Jeffers

Anita's Story

Anita's parents survived the Depression, and they had vivid memories of what it meant to struggle to make ends meet. They continually relived this period of their lives by telling doom-and-gloom stories to their children. Their noble intent was to teach the kids the importance of having a good job that would provide stability and security in their lives.

Their daughter, Anita, was different from everyone else in the family. She loved to perform. Her favorite pastimes were watching TV and going to movies, where she became good at mimicking her favorite characters. In school, she volunteered to be in all the plays and loved hamming it up whenever there was an opportunity to have an audience. Her parents saw this fun-loving, creative and artistic side to Anita but discouraged it because they feared she would spend the rest of her life struggling to be successful. To them, acting was not a real job, and they expected her to go to college and study business so that she could find a stable job that paid a lot of money.

Anita's older brother was the pride and joy of the family. He earned excellent grades in school and had recently been accepted at a reputable law school. Anita's parents often told her that they wished she would be more level-headed, down-to-earth and serious about life like her brother. Anita resented this comparison, which caused a lot of friction between her and her brother. They were different and she knew she could never be like him.

Anita's parents made it clear that they would only send her to college if she majored in business. When she enrolled, she wanted to please her parents, and she also wanted to prove to herself that she could handle classes like accounting, economics and math. But after two years of struggling in these classes, her grades dropped so low that she was dismissed from school. Anita's fragile ego took a devastating blow and her only choice was to look for a job.

After two years of going from one boring job to another and feeling like a failure, Anita's life seemed empty and going nowhere. Meanwhile, her brother graduated from law school and was becoming successful in his practice, which only worsened her low self-esteem. Anita's desperation finally manifested itself in a dependency on drugs and alcohol that drove her to seek help.

Anita says her life began to change the day she entered a substance abuse treatment program. In the process of becoming clean and sober, she finally realized that she had gotten off her true path by trying to please her parents. As she became aware that her fear of losing her parent's approval had caused her struggles, she concluded that her survival depended on doing the work she loved.

After finding a job to support herself, Anita enrolled in acting classes at a local community college. These classes truly made her heart sing as she began to recover her self-esteem and a sense of who she was. Through contacts, she landed a better job with a company that trained her to give seminars to motivate people and teach them how to use the company's product. She had fun doing her new work, and her ability to be comfortable in front of an audience made her an exceptional trainer. Although it was not an acting job, the seminar work was enjoyable enough to sustain her. She continued her acting classes at night.

Anita enjoyed school so much that she not only earned her bachelor's degree but continued on to graduate school and received a master's degree in fine arts, specializing in theater. She is now happier than she has ever been in her life. She supports herself by teaching college students who want to become actors, and performs in community playhouses at night. Anita feels passionate about inspiring other creative people to pursue their dreams, while she also makes a living doing what she loves to do. Her goal is not to become rich and famous, although she thinks it would be great to be so fortunate. Her mission is to use her gifts and talents to serve others through her ability to teach and entertain.

Anita's fear initially prevented her from doing the work she loved, but by selling out to please her parents she created the gloom and doom and instability they hoped she would avoid. Her decision to listen to her own inner voice turned her life around.

Because Anita's Orange personality thrives on creativity, freedom of expression, spontaneity, fun and excitement, her choice to teach acting and perform serves as a perfect outlet for her gifts. Orange characteristics are part of her true nature, and her peace of mind and success depend on her acknowledging and expressing them. Her parents are both Gold personalities, who need and value something different. Golds want security, stability and predictability in their lives. A traditional job that pays well, has a good health plan and provides retirement benefits is important to them. Golds will likely be the most unsettled by our changing times, when most of us can no longer depend on traditional benefits in our jobs.

Anita's story is not unusual. Many people struggle before discovering the track that provides meaning and purpose to their lives. Looking at relationships between parents and children sheds some light on the source of much of our fear and confusion.

Ideally, parents would see each child as someone who was born to make a special contribution to society in a unique way, and who already possesses inherent personality gifts for expressing who he is. It's no accident that one person has a particular talent and another has a different one. One is not better than another (although society imposes different values), they are just different! We have these gifts for a reason and the best way to enjoy our work is to use them. The most frustrated people I know are those who are wasting their precious gifts because they don't understand how they are unique and special.

If parents viewed their children as uniquely gifted, they would nurture and support the natural potential in each one; they would see who their children truly are and would encourage them to follow the directions of their inner selves to discover their unique life's work; they would accept and validate their children's unique traits and would not try to mold them into what they want them to be.

In such a positive environment, children would grow up with a better understanding of their natural gifts and talents, and who they are. They would have higher self-esteem, confidence and an awareness of how they want to express their own uniqueness.

Unfortunately, most of us were not raised in this ideal manner, and we may be making similar mistakes with our own kids. Most parents do the best they can to raise their children with the knowledge they have at the time. The good news is that we can break this vicious cycle. We can accept, acknowledge and validate our own uniqueness and the uniqueness of others. We can become a society that produces happy and responsible people who are conscious of who they are and what gifts they have to offer the world.

Start with yourself. Once you understand and appreciate your own unique blend of talents, gifts and interests, and once you recognize the natural ways you prefer to express yourself, you can apply your new insight to other people and realize that everyone has a natural combination of gifts that makes them who they are. This stunning revelation will allow you to let go of blame and misunderstanding and begin to see the world from another perspective. At the same time, you can strengthen your own expression of your built-in personality and begin to move in the direction of your life's work.

In Anita's case, it made sense that her Gold parents would value a business degree, which was too restrictive for an Orange like Anita. But once Anita discovered her true colors and began to follow her true self, her parents were able to see and appreciate her natural strengths. Anita was able to forgive her parents' misguided efforts in raising her, and everyone ultimately understood each other better. Best of all, Anita was blossoming in her life's work.

Another parental pitfall is when parents try to live out their own unfulfilled dreams through their children. Jason and his father shared similar values. They both were primary Orange personalities — Jason was Orange-Blue and his father was Orange-Green, but they had different visions for their lives. Jason's father was a high school football star who wanted to play professionally, but because of a knee injury he was unable to actualize his dreams. Consequently, as Jason was growing up, his father pushed him to participate in sports. Jason felt he didn't have the necessary athletic skills and he also was not interested in sports.

What Jason did love was playing the guitar, and he would practice long hours after school. His father never supported him and accused him of being a sissy, but for Jason nothing else gave him the same passion and satisfaction as his music. When he began to have problems in school, his high school counselor intervened and showed his father how his pressure on Jason to play sports was the cause of Jason's problems. Today, Jason feels he owes his success as a musician to his counselor, because without her help he thinks he would have been totally discouraged from playing his music.

Our kids are always giving us clues about who they are. Although Jason and his father were both spontaneous, fun-loving and extroverted personalities, his father was physically inclined while Jason was more artistically creative. Sometimes we can see so much of ourselves in our children that we miss who they truly are if we don't look for their uniqueness. If Jason's father had paid attention, he would have seen that Jason's natural potential was in his music and not his athletic ability.

Parental roles would be more productive if we would observe what our children naturally gravitate toward, and encourage them instead of forcing our own visions.

Looking back and examining your relationship with your parents may unlock great insights to help you understand what was important to them, how this may have been different from what was important to you, and what influence this had on your career choices. Reread the color chapters that represent your parents. Use the following exercise to assist you.

Sentence Completion Exercise

1. My father's primary (first) color is _____
   (If he is deceased, talking to someone who knew him better than you could be helpful.)

2. Some of the most important things (values) my father cared about were _____
   _____
   (Reading the chapter on your father's primary color or the values listed for his color in chapter Nine can be helpful.)

3. The major clash between what my father cares about and what is important to me is _____
   _____

4. My father acknowledged me for _____
   _____

5. What I want him to acknowledge and validate me for is
   _____

6. The impact this has had on my life and career decisions is
   _____
   _____

1. My mother's primary (first) color is _____ -
   (If she is deceased, talking to someone who knew her
   better than you could be helpful.)

2. Some of the most important things (values) my mother
   cared about were _____
   (Reading the chapter on your mother's primary color or
   the values listed for her color in chapter Nine can be
   helpful.)

3. The major clash between what my mother cares about and
   what is important to me is _____
   _____

4. My mother acknowledged me for _____
   _____

5. What I want her to acknowledge and validate me for is
   _____
   _____

6. The impact this has had on my life and career decisions is
   _____

Ask yourself these questions:

1. As a child, what did I fantasize about doing when I grew up?
2. What feelings did this fantasy conjure up inside of me?
3. Who supported my dreams?
4. Who discouraged me?
5. Has my fantasy changed?
6. If so, what is my current fantasy?
7. Who are my role models?
8. How close is my fantasy to what I am doing at work each day?
9. What would it take for me to live my fantasy?
10. What would I have to give up?
11. How much am I willing to sacrifice in order to live my fantasy?
12. What is it costing me not to live my fantasy? Health? Happiness? Peace of mind? Is it worth it?

Are you moving in a direction toward instead of away from your goals and dreams? If your answer is "no," ask yourself why not. This could be a difficult question to answer because you may be unconsciously sabotaging your success. Research shows that messages received early in life can continue to affect your actions, thoughts and feelings as an adult. When these messages are negative they can become life scripts that develop into repeated patterns which prevent you from achieving your goals.

If you don't like the "scripts" given to you during your childhood, you can rewrite them. As an adult you can choose to live your life any way you want. Your true self has always been inside of you, although it may have been hidden and obscured by your fears. To reach your potential you must be willing to let who you are shine.

If we look at the negative scripts given to Anita by her parents they would sound something like this:

It's not okay to be spontaneous and carefree.
You should be more serious about life.
It's not important to enjoy your work — making money is more
    important.
Acting is not a real job.
If you don't do what I say you will be a failure.
You should be more like your brother.
Who you are is not good enough.

If Anita rewrote her scripts she could imagine her parents saying something like this:

You are unique and special and there is no one else like you.
We love your spontaneous and carefree nature.
It's a joy to see you play and have fun.
It's important for you to enjoy your work.
Acting is a perfect way for you to express who you are.
You will be successful if you follow your own path.
Never imitate anyone else.
It's important to be who you are and we love you the way you
    are.

Rewrite Your Scripts

Practice rewriting your own scripts by first listing some of the negative messages given to you as you were growing up

1.

2.

3.

4.

5.

6.

7.

Now rewrite your scripts by changing these negative messages into positive ones. As an adult, take responsibility for bringing your true colors out into the open and begin to regard them in a positive light. It may be helpful to tape-record your scripts and listen to them before going to bed at night. Hearing these positive messages before falling asleep can have a powerful impact on your mind.

1.

2.

3.

4.

5.

6.

7.

As you uncover your true self and begin to follow your dream, eventually you will encounter the big, bad dream buster — fear. Fear is sneaky and can appear in many forms. There's fear of change, fear of failure and success, fear of disapproval from your parents or spouse or others, fear of the power of your natural abilities, fear of whatever you choose to fear.

Fortunately, fear can be banished by three powerful elements: light, action and faith. Remember when you were a kid and the shadows in your room at night made you pull the covers up around your neck? How did you banish your fear of the dark? You turned on the light. In a similar way, discovering your true colors shines a light on your inner self and illumines your natural gifts and interests. You can also now see what you're not — and what you no longer have to pretend to be. What a relief! Self-knowledge is a bright light.

Action is another effective antidote for fear. In her book, *Feel the Fear and Do it Anyway*, Dr. Susan Jeffers says the only way to get rid of fear is to do whatever we're afraid of. When you take action you confront your fear and it goes away. In the process you also develop your skills and build your self-esteem. Anyone who is successful has had to confront fear. Everyone feels fear, but successful people do not let fear deter them from following their dreams and reaching their goals.

Faith opposes fear, but in order to utilize faith we must first understand it. Faith must have an object, and your faith is only as valid as its object. When you place your faith in your true colors, you are trusting the way you were created to be. As you develop your natural gifts and talents and pursue your natural interests, you will grow in confidence and overcome your fear. You might also have faith in God or faith in others to help you along the way to making your unique contribution to the world.

Nothing better describes the breakthrough I had with my own fear than the following excerpt from Nelson Mandela's 1994 Inaugural address.

Our deepest fear is not that we are inadequate,
Our deepest fear is that we are powerful beyond measure.
It is our light, not our darkness, that most frightens us.
We ask ourselves, who am I to be brilliant, gorgeous,
talented and fabulous?
Actually, who are you not to be?
You are a child of God.
Your playing small doesn't serve the world.
There's nothing enlightened about shrinking so that
other people won't feel insecure around you.
We were born to make manifest the glory of God that is within
us.
It's not in some of us; it's in everyone.
And as we let our own light shine, we unconsciously
give other people permission to do the same.
As we are liberated from our own fear,
our presence automatically liberates others.

Changing your thinking can change your life. The next chapter will show you how your thoughts create your experiences and will give you steps you can take to change your thinking in order to create your ideal life's work.

11

How to Create Your Ideal Life's Work

‹ ‹ ‹ ‹ ‹ ‹ ‹ ‹ ‹ ‹ ‹ ‹ › › › › › › › › › › › ›

Whatever the mind can conceive and believe it can achieve.

Napoleon Hill
Think and Grow Rich

Now that you have made some decisions about the work you love to do and faced your fear, it is time to use the power of your mind to make your dreams come true. This chapter will require you to draw on all four parts of your personality — Green, Blue, Orange and Gold — to create your ideal life's work and be successful. You will be given six steps to follow and told which color, or set of personality strengths, will help you with each one. If that particular color happens to be your first, which represents your major strengths, the skills needed should be familiar and easy for you to apply. Some steps will draw on weaker parts of your personality and may present more of a challenge.

Remember we are all good at some things and not others. Accepting our personality differences while seeking to build on our strengths makes life more enjoyable for everyone. The idea is not to focus on your weaknesses but to manage them so that you are not crippled by them. It is important that you do not try to turn a weakness into a strength. It would be a total waste of your time.

You may want to use other people who have the strengths of a particular primary color as your coaches or mentors. Ask them to help you improve in areas where you are weak. They can tell you what works for them. I don't think they will say no, because most people love talking about their favorite subject — themselves!

The philosophy behind the True Colors system is consistent with the research done by Abraham Maslow, who studied self-actualized people. Rather than using the traditional medical model, which focuses on disease or what is wrong with people, Maslow paid attention to what was right and healthy in individuals. He studied the moments when people felt happy, accomplished and fulfilled. In his attempt to learn how our minds work, he discovered what goes on in the minds of people when they are at their best.

Maslow called these highest moments, when you feel fully actualized, "peak experiences." Some of the qualities of a peak experience include feelings of being more yourself, while simultaneously merging with whatever activity you're involved in; utilizing all your greatest capabilities easily and effortlessly; feelings of being totally present and in the moment, as though there is no place else you would rather be; and a sense of spontaneity and playfulness. You may have had a peak experience when you first learned to ride a bicycle or drive a car, spoke with ease in front of an audience, competed in a race, or played a successful game of tennis.

One of Maslow's most important discoveries was that during these peak experiences people are taking directions from their inner selves rather than from the outside world. They pay attention to people and situations around them, but self-actualized people tend to trust their inner guidance more. You might say they rely on their treasures within.

Take the following steps to help you rely on your own inner guidance in creating your ideal life's work.

Step One: Take Responsibility for Your Life

Your first step in changing your life is to decide to take responsibility for having what you want. You can draw on the Gold part of your personality to assist in making this move. Golds are good at making decisions and sticking with them until completion of a project. If you are not satisfied with the work you do, rewrite your script by choosing something different. You're in charge of your life, so make it look the way you want. Choose your own outcomes.

To do this you must first accept that you are responsible for your beliefs and actions. Self-actualized people already know this and look to their inner selves to guide them. The intention of this book is to help you take an inward journey to understand what you need in your work to make you happy and successful. Now it is time to put this information into practice by creating the work you love to do.

In his book *The Seven Habits of Highly Effective People*, Steven Covey calls taking responsibility Habit Number One. He says that productive people do not blame their behavior on the circumstances and conditions in their lives. They do not make excuses for why their lives aren't working. Those who allow other things to control them are being reactive, not proactive. Proactive people take control and do whatever is necessary to accomplish their goals.

It is difficult to feel good about yourself when you give your power away by making something or someone else responsible for your life. This condition will only keep you stuck with low self-esteem and feeling like a failure. To be an effective person who is successfully doing your life's work, you must decide to take responsibility for your life. Tell yourself it is time to commit to making this positive change in your life.

Step Two: Have a Strong Desire for Your Vision

Your mission statement was designed to help you clarify the purpose of your life. Now it is time to use the Green part of you to stay focused on your vision. Greens are visionaries who use the limitless power of their minds to achieve their desires, and so can you. Napoleon Hill, author of *Think and Grow Rich*, says, "Henry Ford was a success because he understood and applied the principles of success. One of these was desire, knowing what you want."

Knowing what you want is not the same as wishing and hoping for something to happen. Those who only hope and wish for things don't have much faith in their own power to create what they want. Instead, you must have a desire to be and do all that you are capable of. Being is a state of staying true to who you are. Doing is using your natural gifts and talents to make whatever is important to you happen. To be successful in your life's work, you must keep your desire in alignment with your true self and you must know that you can have what you want. Reviewing your mission statement and your life's work choice daily will help you stay focused on your vision.

The next step is to set your intention. Author Gary Zukav, in *The Seat of the Soul*, says, "You create your reality with your intentions." That is, when we strongly desire something and totally believe we can have it — and make it our intention to do so — our minds will assist us in creating what we desire. If this concept sounds strange or contrived, consider this: you already create your reality with your intentions every day, consciously or otherwise. For example, most of us make it our intention to take a daily shower, get to work on time and eat a certain number of meals. We don't spend a lot of time thinking about these things, but we remember to do them because it is our intention to do so. This is how intentions work, once we have decided what we want. We can do the same to create our ideal work.

Start by writing a clear and specific vision statement about the life's work you intend to create, and set a date by which you will accomplish this goal. Example: "I am working successfully as a motivational speaker by December, 1998." Read this statement first thing every morning and every evening before going to sleep. Saying it in the morning will keep you focused on it during your waking hours and repeating it at night will allow your mind to entertain the thought while you're sleeping.

If this step seems impractical, imagine what our modern world would be like if Thomas Edison, the Wright brothers and Albert Einstein had not been great dreamers and visionaries. Whether inventing the light bulb, launching an airplane or creating a new theory, each of these men started with an idea and a dream mixed with a strong desire to create their vision.

You too can use your powerful mind to create your vision, and rely on your strong desire to keep you focused until it materializes.

Step Three: Develop a Positive Mental Attitude

Take a "Yes I Can" attitude and stay focused on what is positive about yourself. To assist you in this step, draw from the Blue part of your personality or let a Blue help you. Blues like to think positively and see the best in everyone.

How capable are you of having the successful life's work you desire? Ralph Waldo Emerson said, "A man becomes what he thinks about most of the time." What do you think about yourself most of the time? You cannot expect to be any better or more successful than your self-concept. Your self-concept is different from your self-esteem. Whereas self-esteem is emotional — how you feel about yourself, self-concept is cognitive — what you believe about yourself. What you believe about yourself, positively or negatively, will reflect from the inside out and be expressed in your behavior.

Don't worry about fixing your behavior. Focusing on behavior is the equivalent of putting a bandage on a wound. Instead, change the inside. When you heal the inside, the outside will automatically take care of itself. That is what is meant by the saying, "as within, so without."

We constantly repeat things to ourselves in our minds, but if what we repeat is consistently negative, these thoughts can be destructive. Fortunately, much like installing a new program on a computer to achieve a different outcome, you can do the same with your mind. A powerful technique to change self-deprecating thoughts to positive is to use affirmations. Positive statements declare that something is already happening. Key point: this is not a one-size-fits-all program. Some positive statements are universal, but others need to be more specific. The power of True Colors is to anchor your positive statements in the natural strengths and talents that already undergird your personality. A Gold will focus on different positive traits than an Orange or a Blue or a Green. If True Colors has opened your eyes the way it did mine, you suddenly have a treasure chest full of gems — positive attributes that compose your primary color — that you can use to bolster a positive self-concept.

Napoleon Hill says, "Every man is what he is because of the dominating thoughts which he permits to occupy his mind." What dominant thoughts are you holding on to about yourself? Positive self-talk rooted in the truth about your inner self can force you to take control of your mind and think about what you want to think about.

The purpose of affirmations is to help you have what you want by being who you are and doing what you want to do. But because people are typically resistant to change, this will require time and patience. Many say it takes twenty-one days to change a habit, but that's not bad for something you may have been doing for a lifetime. Regardless of how much time it takes, be persistent until positive results show in your behavior without your consciously thinking about it. When you no longer have to think about it, you will know the change is real. It is worth working and waiting for something that permanently changes your life.

Use the examples below of positive self-talk to create your own list of affirmations that fit who you truly are. Make your statements in the present tense and the positive voice. For example, say, "I am healthy," rather than, "I don't want to be sick."

It's a joy to get up every morning and do my life's work.

I am being all that I am capable of being.

I use my natural, God-given talents in my work.

I love myself unconditionally.

I am happy and enjoying life.

My work is mentally stimulating.

I am loving and compassionate toward others.

My life is filled with loving, kind and supportive people.

I use the creative ideas that constantly flow through my mind.

I use my time wisely.

My work is fun and exciting.

I have all the money I need to live the lifestyle that I desire.

My life is successful.

Step Four: Visualize Your Ideal Life's Work

The image you have of yourself determines whether or not you will be successful. If your self-image doesn't represent who you are capable of being, the good news is that you can change it. Visualize yourself doing your life's work. Trust your intuition — the knowledge that goes beyond your five senses. Use your imagination. It is very powerful. Albert Einstein said, "Imagination is more important than knowledge." He also said that intuition is more valuable than facts.

Blues are natural dreamers. If Blue isn't your primary color, ask a Blue to coach you in this process.

Remember, all change is from the inside out. To create a new concept and image of yourself, you must begin by changing your mental picture. The circumstances in your life will then automatically conform to this new image.

See yourself in your mind already doing your life's work. If you have never attempted to use this technique, it may seem odd at first, but many successful people are using it to create their dreams. Sports figures often visualize themselves shooting a ball into a basket, hitting a golf ball into the right hole, or scoring a touchdown in their own minds before they actually do it in real life. The internal, visual picture they create is what they later reproduce during a game.

The rear brain cannot distinguish between something imagined and something actually happening, which is why your heart races and you break out in a cold sweat if you think there is a burglar in your house, even if you discover it's only an unexpected family member. Your unconscious mind responds the same as it would to an actual burglar. Your mind is a source of power you can tap into to create whatever you want in life.

Visualization is a powerful tool you can use to create what you want. You may want to utilize the following steps to help you. To begin the process, it is important to decide what you want your life and work to look like. Use these questions to assist you.

What would a typical work day look like?
What time do you get up?
How are you dressed?
What does your home look like?
Who else lives there?
What kind of car do you drive?
What time do you get to work?
What does your office look like?
What are the people you work with like?
What do you do all day?
What time do you leave the office?
How do you feel at the end of the day?
How much money do you make?

Sit quietly and relax your body. Slow down your breathing to calm yourself. Breathe in to the count of five, hold your breath to the count of five, then exhale to the count of five. Repeat this exercise five times or until you feel calm.

Create a clear picture in your mind of exactly the way you want your life and work to be. See yourself on a typical day doing what you love to do. The more real you can make the picture, with specific details and specific positive feelings, the better your chance of creating exactly what you want. Use the questions above to help you.

Repeat your affirmations from Step Three to stay focused and keep your mind from wandering.

Feel gratitude and acknowledge yourself for your accomplishment. Although this exercise took place entirely in your mind, imagine feeling the way you would if it happened in real life and think of it as being completed.

Use this process as long as you need to accomplish your goals, but don't force it — that would only hinder your progress.

Step Five: Set Goals

This step will make all the other ones work. When I learned how much my vision, desires, dreams, happiness and success in life all depended on this step, I made it an important habit in my life. When I review a list I wrote months or years ago, I am amazed at how many of my goals I have accomplished.

Goal setting is where you separate yourself from those who only talk about what they want. You are now ready to join the group of exceptional people who actually make things happen, leaving behind those who wonder what happened to their lives.

You'll need to allow your Gold self, that part of you that knows how to take responsibility for making decisions and carrying them out, to take the lead in this step. If Gold is not your first color and especially if it is your last color, you may need to use a Gold coach to help you with this step.

Successful people set goals. They don't wish for, hope for or allow things to happen to them at random. Without goals you go through life reacting rather than focusing. It's like going to the supermarket without knowing what you want. There are so many choices that you may not get what you need, and will probably take longer than necessary to shop. If you have goals (or a shopping list in our example), you can still be flexible enough to add appropriate elements as you go (the occasional impulse purchase), but your main effort will be to get what you need. Goals provide clarity about what you want and determine the direction of your decisions, rather than leaving things to happen inadvertently. Setting goals can be the catalyst you need to begin your success.

You are where you are today because of decisions you have made. If you don't like where you are, you need to make decisions more deliberately. Goals put you in charge. Take advantage of this step to give the vision for your life's work the best chance of actualizing. Your mind is capable of seeing that you accomplish your goals, but you need to be clear about what you want. If your desire is strong, and your effort is persistent, you will achieve your objectives. Don't be like most people and give up too soon.

Your outer world mirrors your inner thoughts and desires. In *Think and Grow Rich*, Napoleon Hill says, "Truly, thoughts are things, and powerful things at that when they are mixed with definiteness of purpose, persistence, and a burning desire for their translation into riches, or other material objects." Thinking about your goals will attract the right people, ideas and circumstances into your life to make you successful.

You can use the guidelines below to help you set your goals.

- Make your life mission your main purpose or major goal in life. All other goals can be organized around this one.
- Write your goals down. Mark Victor Hansen, co-author of *Chicken Soup for the Soul*, says, "As soon as you think it — ink it!" Writing your goals makes them concrete and puts energy behind them. You can then look at your list daily.
- Think of your goal list with an unlimited mindset: If you could be and do anything you want, what would your life look like? Think of how others would also benefit from your vision. It may include such things as eliminating

poverty, hunger and homelessness; creating world peace; or curing diseases.

- Make a list of 100 or more goals. It's better to have too many goals than too few as long as you don't try to do them all at once.

- Decide which goals can be accomplished within one month, six months, or one year, and which will take five years or longer.

- Set a deadline for each goal. Remember, deadlines can be changed, but it's important to have one initially in mind. This allows your mind to think in terms of completion.

- Always acknowledge yourself whenever you accomplish a goal. Pat yourself on the back, pause and celebrate. Take time out to do something special for yourself. You deserve it!

Step Six: Take Action

You already know everything you need to in order to make your dreams a reality. The only question now is: Are you willing to make it happen? Draw on your Orange traits to muster the energy and excitement needed to put your plan into action. If necessary, find a primary Orange to coach you.

You began these steps by taking responsibility and having a strong desire to create your ideal life's work, but to finish them you have to be persistent. You must not allow your mind to entertain the thought of quitting. If you give up and "keep on doing what you've been doing, you'll keep on getting what you've been getting." Ask yourself whether getting up every morning and doing what you do every day is all there is to life. If your answer is no, make the decision to do something different now — not someday.

You may be tempted to put things off until some future date "when the time is right." Unfortunately, there will never be such a time. Life goes on and there will always be obstacles to interfere with your plans, but don't let that stop you. If you stay focused on making your dreams come true, things have a way of working out the way they are supposed to. Trust yourself. When you make the decision that nothing will stop you, nothing will. Never give up and you will be successful.

Doing something that you feel passionate about creates an incredible amount of energy and enthusiasm. To keep this momentum going, do something related to your vision every day — even if it's a small thing like reading your list of goals. Daily action will keep you motivated and positive about your plans. Only you can make your dreams happen. If you can dream it you can do it!

Believe in Yourself

You are your own greatest asset —
there is nothing you cannot do.
No one can keep you from dreaming
your dreams, and only you can
prevent them from coming true.
Your achievements are not
determined by your ability alone,
but by the desire you possess
to reach them. There are no worlds
outside of those you create for
yourself, and the only
boundaries are those you
establish and choose to live within.
Never be afraid to defend your
decisions, regardless. No one can
possibly know what is best for you
other than yourself.

Terry Everton*

12

The Harmony of Colors

‹ ‹ ‹ ‹ ‹ ‹ ‹ ‹ ‹ ‹ ‹ ‹ ‹ › › › › › › › › › › › ›

I see your true colors shining through.
I see your true colors and that's why I love you.
So don't be afraid to let them show...
Your true colors are beautiful like a rainbow.

from the song *True Colors*
by Cindy Lauper

Imagine a world where everyone lives and works in harmony, expressing the human diversity found in all four personalities. I envision a place where everyone knows who he or she is and accepts others as individuals who have different, yet equally important, personality strengths and talents. They don't compete with each other because they know that each person is unique and has a special contribution to make in his or her own way. Everyone's gifts are needed and utilized.

One way to begin to create this kind of ideal world is in our work life. We can think of it as one of the many games we play in life. Like any other game, the better we understand it the better we will play. This book is about playing the career game, or what

I ultimately call the game of life's work. Success in your work can also have a positive effect on other areas of your life.

Most important, you must understand that in this game there are no losers — only winners. Because the goal is to do what you love, the only way to lose is to drop out and choose not to play at all, or settle for a job to pay the bills. Those who decide to play this game know that each one has a special role which cannot be carried out by anyone else. There is no one else exactly like you.

Mastering the game of life's work requires a paradigm shift. If you think of work with the same old business-as-usual attitude, you will continue to get the same results. But if you're not happy with your present work, a new approach will be refreshing and potentially life-changing. The following major points form the core of this new view of work.

Have a Purpose

Everything begins with a purpose, and without one life has no meaning. Decide what your purpose is or life will seem like a confusing, frustrating and meaningless journey. How can you be sure that what you're doing is not a waste of time if there is no standard of measure?

The key to success in the game of life's work is knowing your purpose in life. The life mission statement you wrote in chapter Nine answers the question of why you perform the tasks you do. If what you presently do is not consistent with this statement, you need to reassess your involvement. It is paramount that your purpose be aligned with expressing who you are and using your natural gifts and talents to do what you love.

Know How to Play

Games are designed to be fun, and when you do what you love, it is fun. Let go of any conditioning that says life is hard and you have to struggle, or the belief that work cannot be fun. Exchange your concept of working hard for one of "working well." Technology has eliminated most hard labor so that we can work smarter. When you work smart, you use your natural gifts and talent, and what used to be a struggle becomes an invigorating challenge. How hard is it to be who you are and do what you do best? Hard work is doing something you're not good at that you don't like.

Our work ethic in this country discourages us from playing by making us believe it is frivolous and a waste of time. The traditional attitude toward work promotes making sacrifices, expending effort and being serious. Look at the faces of most people at work. They look miserable — certainly not alive. If the traditional view is such a good idea, why do so many people hate their jobs?

Play is natural, but so many of us have forgotten how to play. Some people who have bought into a strong work ethic cannot even enjoy playing for the sake of playing. I observed this phenomenon while bike-riding with a friend. It turned into such hard work with so many rules, shoulds, and seriousness that I couldn't participate. What was the point? It wasn't fun anymore. If I wanted to work that hard I could be like everybody else and get a job I hate. At least then I could say I was getting paid to be miserable.

Play on a Win-Win Basis

When you do what you do best and I do what I do best, everybody wins. You don't have to fail for me to succeed. Competition only breeds jealousy. But if I know that we can both win, I can use my time and energy productively by helping other people win, and the only person I need to compete with is myself — always striving to do what I do even better. Competition with yourself is healthy.

Know the Ingredients for Success

- You must know who you are to play your role. Your life's work needs to be compatible with your true self.
- You must know your strengths as well as your weaknesses. Then you can look for work that utilizes what you do best rather than taxing your weaker skills and creating a lot of stress.
- You must have a means to carry out your purpose. Will you have a title, such as president, teacher or lawyer, or will you volunteer your time to an area of interest? Some choose the position of homemaker or caretaker. The outlet you choose must allow you to express your purpose.
- Recognize and respect individual differences. People will play the game differently and that's okay. There is no single script for how to play. Who you are will determine how you play your best.

Understand the Role of Each Player

This game has four types of players, Green, Blue, Gold and Orange, and each has natural gifts and talents to play the role for which he is best suited. Strengths and abilities are not equally shared, yet each is aware of his own uniqueness, while respecting the same in others. Each makes a contribution in his own special way.

The Green Player

Without vision we cannot survive. We can rely on our Green players to provide vision to keep us growing and moving in a positive direction. Their innovative ideas, depth of knowledge and profound wisdom will constantly challenge the rest of us to raise our own consciousness of what our world could be rather than settling for what is comfortable and familiar.

The Blue Player

We can count on our Blue players to be our harmonizers. Their strong desire to have us all get along with each other will force us to look for peaceful means of settling our conflicts. Regardless of their specific life's work, their love and support will comfort us in our effort to be the best we can be.

The Gold Player

Our Gold players are the stabilizers of our society who will prevent us from living in chaos. Whether at home, work, school or any other setting, they will see to it that things get done in an orderly manner. We can count on them to fill in the details required to make things happen.

The Orange Player

We sometimes forget to enjoy our journey, and we can count on our Orange players to remind us that life is meant to be fun. Whether they make us laugh, sing, dance or exercise our bodies, we can all profit from their attitude as a stress buster to keep us from taking life too seriously. Whatever their position, they bring a lighter touch.

Awareness of the role of each player allows us to work together as a team to accomplish our personal goals as well as the goals of our organizations. We know who will do the best job based on the skills required to be competent in any particular role. We can alleviate the suffering that goes along with playing out of position. By positioning ourselves and others according to our true colors, we can eliminate much of the stress on the job, which should bolster the productivity of each worker.

Identify a goal

A common goal is to have a happy and successful life, but you need to define what success means to you. For some people it is having all the material goods that make life comfortable, but for others possessions are simply not enough. For the latter group, success may not exclude a rich and comfortable life but the process of accomplishing this goal is much more important. The work they do must have a higher meaning, one that nurtures the soul.

When we know who we are and define our purpose in life, we can choose our work to match this purpose. This allows us to go beyond the surface of satisfying our desires for things like a big house with two cars in the garage and eating dinner out once a week, to doing something that provides deeper meaning to ourselves and others. We develop a sense of interdependence that says we are here to support and serve each other in reaching our potentials and accomplishing our goals.

On a larger scale, mastering this game with a new attitude could affect every aspect of our society and the world as a whole. But first we must change our thinking about those who are not like us. Generally speaking, we don't like that which is different, usually because of a lack of understanding.

Parents have the most problem with kids who are not like them, sometimes referred to as the black sheep of the family. Couples argue with each other about how things are "supposed" to be done — another way of saying "my way is right." At work, we criticize people who don't fit in because they don't behave like everybody else, as though there is only one acceptable way to act.

Different does not mean wrong. The dictionary defines "different" as not the same, or partly or totally unlike in nature. There is no judgment of right or wrong in the word itself. We have attached a negative connotation, but fortunately, what we have created we can change. It is time for us to apply the real meaning of the word "different" by accepting those who are not like us.

A new understanding of who we are would demand major changes in systems that affect all our lives, including the two systems that have the most influence in molding our personalities: the family and education. Without making changes in these systems we will continue to produce people who don't understand themselves and are critical of differences in others.

Families have the most impact on shaping our personalities. A child learns more during the first five years of life than any other five-year period. Virginia Satir, the psychologist and author known as "the mother of self-esteem," calls parents "people-makers" because they in effect determine the kind of adult each child becomes. Satir says that "troubled families make troubled people and thus contribute to the devaluing of self, which is linked to crime, mental illness, alcoholism, drug abuse, poverty, alienated youth, terrorism, and many other social problems." We cannot talk about changing individuals without changing the system that produces these individuals.

Parents need training on how to raise happy, healthy children who become adults who feel good about themselves. Most parents raise their children based on how their own parents raised them. If the model they got from their parents was unhealthy, then what they pass on to their children will also be an unhealthy model of parenting. The only way to break this chain is by educating parents. What was appropriate when they were children may be outdated by the time they become parents, and they need to know how to raise their children according to the current societal norms.

Many of my friends agree that being a parent is the hardest job they have ever had. Yet nobody trained us to do the job. This role is much too important in shaping human lives to be left to on-the-job training. No successful company would hire anyone and expect them to do a good job without some training. Doesn't the job of parenting deserve the same respect?

The following excerpt from a poem on children by the wise poet, Kahlil Gibran, sheds a lot of light on the understanding of parenting that could create happy, healthy children.

Your children are not your children.
They are the sons and daughters of Life's longing
  for itself.
They come through you but not from you,
And though they are with you, yet they belong not
  to you.
You may give them your love but not your thoughts.
For they have their own thoughts.
You may house their bodies but not their souls,
For their souls dwell in the house of tomorrow,
  which you cannot visit, not even in your dreams.
You may strive to be like them, but seek not to make
  them like you.

Education is the other system that has the most influence on shaping our lives. The California Task Force to Promote Self-Esteem concluded that "schools that feature self-esteem as a clearly stated component of their goals, policies and practices are more successful academically as well as in developing healthy self-esteem." If we know this, why aren't we promoting self-esteem in schools? As a preventive method it could be effective in resolving much of our failure and drop-out problems.

The health of a community depends on how healthy the individuals are in that community. Those people who are taught self-esteem at home and at school become healthy members of society. They become the bankers, teachers, ministers and politicians. These are the people who will show up for work and be prepared to do a good job to serve others. As we move more and more toward having technology do much of our work in a society that is service-oriented, it is vitally important that people be interested in serving others.

Individuals with more self-esteem and self-worth produce a society where people enjoy happier and more productive lives. When we appreciate our own uniqueness and self-worth we can accept that others deserve the same respect. We all have something positive to contribute to the world. Others have to be appreciated for their special strengths and talents and allowed to make their unique contributions.

My world vision includes political leaders who are individuals with such high self-esteem that they behave out of respect and love for themselves and other people. They no longer need to use competition, dominance, force or power to control others, but strive to work together as a team. They relate to each other through cooperation and acceptance of individual differences, while embracing our sameness as human beings. A result of this shift in our thinking about who we are could produce major positive changes in our daily behavior.

There would be less physical and verbal abuse of children by parents, because much of the conflict that leads to abuse in families comes from a lack of understanding and appreciation of individual differences. Parents would know how to look for the special qualities in their children and celebrate their uniqueness. Children would feel loved and validated for who they are and grow up with the confidence to actualize their potential.

Schools would be a place where children could enjoy learning and have no desire to drop out. They would feel understood because teachers would also see the uniqueness in them and support and encourage their positive strengths. The role of the school would be to reinforce the self-esteem that children get from their parents. The belief that "no one cares" would no longer be the number one reason why kids drop out of school.

Relationships would work better and divorce rates would consequently drop, because couples would marry for the right reasons. Each would see the other for who he or she truly is and know that the purpose of the marriage relationship is to love and support their individual growth and self-discovery together. Neither would feel the need to change partners, because they would recognize the uniqueness that needs to be expressed. Each would give the other the freedom to reach his or her own potential.

We would have careers that lead to our life's work instead of merely holding down jobs. With our validation from home and school we would know who we are and what we are supposed to do with our lives. Our work would simply be a way to get paid to express our natural gifts and talents. We would then feel a sense of fulfillment as we provided a needed service to others. The workplace would draw from all four personalities working together as a team.

Ultimately, we would build better communities and a better world, because when people have self-esteem they don't need to have everyone else be like them to feel comfortable. We would understand and accept individuals of all races and cultures as human beings first and their differences as part of their God-given uniqueness. This new paradigm would be one of acceptance of human diversity which transcends our limited view of cultural diversity. Culture is learned; our individual uniqueness is who we truly are. We would finally make peace with each other, and when we spoke of a person's color, it would have nothing to do with her skin pigmentation. We would recognize, understand and appreciate their True Colors.

Love Them Anyway

(a favorite of the beloved Mother Teresa)

1.   People are illogical, unreasonable, and self-centered. Love them anyway.
2.   If you do good, people will accuse you of selfish motives. Do good anyway.
3.   If you are successful, you win false friends and true enemies. Succeed anyway.
4.   The good you do may be forgotten tomorrow. Do good anyway.
5.   Honesty and frankness can make you vulnerable. Be honest anyway.
6.   The biggest people with the biggest ideas can be shot down by the smallest people with the smallest ideas. Think big anyway.
7.   People favor underdogs but follow top dogs. Fight for the underdogs anyway.
8.   What you spent years building may be destroyed overnight. Build anyway.
9.   People who need help may attack you if you help them. Help them anyway.
10. Give the world the best you have and you may get kicked in the teeth. Give your best anyway.

Kent Keith*

---

* © Kent M. Keith 1968. (Contact: Kent M. Keith, 2626 Hillside Avenue, Honolulu, HI 96822 USA.)In*The Silent Revolution: Dynamic Leadership in the Student Council,* Harvard Student Agencies, Cambridge, Massachusetts, 1968.

Appendix A

Blues: Some Tips on How Others Can Relate to Them

Do:
1. Tell them what your personal feelings are about any topic
2. Listen attentively and look at them while talking to them
3. Tell them what you appreciate about them
4. Physically touch them (appropriate hugs and kisses)
5. Accept their individuality and uniqueness
6. Allow them to express their feelings
7. Be honest and sincere.

Don't
1. Be abrupt or cut them off while they are talking
2. Discount their dreams
3. Expect them to be confrontational
4. Compare them to someone else
5. Deny their emotions or criticize their sensitivity
6. Ignore them
7. Take advantage of their kindness.

The Kinds of Gifts to Buy Blues

(something personal)
anything with angels on it (candles, stamps, pictures, writing paper)

flowers

chocolate candy

clothes

jewelry

a romantic novel

lingerie

a self-help book

a personal growth seminar

a spiritual retreat
perfume
a candlelight dinner and dancing
a love story video
a subscription to a New Age magazine
a fashion magazine
a romantic or sentimental card
a meditation tape
a gift certificate for a facial
a body massage
body lotion
a poem

Famous Blue Personalities:

Role models are those people who we resonate with because of shared values. We relate to others who are like us. The following list contains famous personalities which Blues have identified as people they relate to.

Abraham Maslow
Annette Funicello
Billy Dee Williams
Carl Jung
Carl Rogers
Christopher Darden
Dinah Shore
Dyan Cannon
Halle Berry
Jack Canfield
Joan Lunden
Julie Andrews
Katie Couric
Leo Buscaglia
Linda Evans
Mariah Carey

Marie Osmond
Mark Hughes
Meg Ryan
Melanie Griffith
Michael Jackson
Mother Teresa
Mr. Rogers
Natalie Wood
Oprah Winfrey
Princess Diana
Ralph Waldo Emerson
Richard Simmons
Sally Field
Sally Jesse Raphael
Sally Struthers
Shirley Temple
Whitney Houston

Understanding the Strengths and Weaknesses of the Blue Boss

Strengths

The strength of Blue bosses is — no surprise — in their people skills. Their style of management is very people-oriented. They will focus their attention on the individuals who work for them and encourage them to reach their own potential. It is their nature to want to draw out the best in others; therefore, they will act more as coaches and mentors toward their workers. Because of their enthusiasm and warmth most people will be willing to cooperate with them. A harmonious environment where people communicate in a positive way and work together as a team is the climate that they will strive to create.

Weaknesses

Blue bosses least favorite things to deal with are conflict and disharmony. In fact, they will go to any length to avoid these situations. This could create a tremendous hardship for them with disgruntled employees. In fact, conflict and terminating undesirable workers are two things that Blue bosses say they dislike most about being the boss. Many avoid the job for these reasons. The exception might be the Blue-Orange boss, who tends to handle confrontation better than other Blues.

Greens: Some Tips on How Others Can Relate to Them

Do:
1. Give logical explanations
2. Allow them time to think about their decisions
3. Expect them to take a leadership role
4. Earn their respect
5. Acknowledge their intelligence
6. Present data to support ideas
7. Recognize their need to get to the point quickly.

Don't:
1. Force them to talk about their feelings too much
2. Become too emotional when arguing with them
3. Be indecisive
4. Expect public display of emotions
5. Take everything they say personally
6. Force them to go to parties
7. Embarrass them in public.

The Kinds of Gifts to Buy Greens

(something mentally stimulating)
    a puzzle
    a computer

tickets to the theater
a chess game
authentic art work
a book on a subject they are interested in
live plants
dinner at an elegant restaurant
a subscription to *Newsweek* magazine or *World News*
antiques
a classical music concert or tape
a camera
a calculator
subscription to the *Wall Street Journal*
a science fiction book
a spy novel
a witty or clever card
something environmentally sound
a globe
the best new dictionary

Famous Green Personalities:

Role models are those people who we resonate with because of shared values. We relate to others who are like us. The following list contains famous personalities which Greens have identified as people they relate to.

Abraham Lincoln
Al Gore
Albert Einstein
Anita Hill
Aristotle
Arnold Schwarzenegger
Barbara Bush
Barbara Walters
Barbra Streisand

Bill Cosby
Bill Gates
Booker T. Washington
Boris Yeltsin
Bryant Gumbel
Candice Bergen
Clarence Thomas
Dick Cavett
Dwight D. Eisenhower
Edgar Allen Poe
George Washington
Gloria Allred
Gloria Steinem
Henry David Thoreau
Henry Kissinger
Hillary Clinton
Jacqueline Kennedy Onassis
James Earl Jones
Jane Fonda
Jane Pauley
Jerry Brown
John Adams
John Bradshaw
John F. Kennedy
Johnny Carson
Johnny Cochran
Larry King
Lee Iacocca
Lily Tomlin
Mohandas Gandhi
Margaret Thatcher
Marcia Clark
Martin Luther King
Maya Angelou
Mikhail Gorbachev
Mr. Spock (from *Star Trek*)

Norman Vincent Peale
Phil Donahue
Plato
Prince Charles
Richard Nixon
Robert Kennedy
Robin Williams
Rosa Parks
Shirley MacLaine
Sidney Poitier
Sigmund Freud
Socrates
Spike Lee
Steve Martin
Steven Spielberg
Susan B. Anthony
Ted Turner
Thomas Jefferson
Thurgood Marshall
Werner Erhart
Whoopi Goldberg
Woody Allen

Understanding the Strengths and Weaknesses of the Green Boss

Strengths

Green bosses have the intellect and confidence of natural born leaders and people see them in this role. The higher the position, the better. In fact, it is easier for them to lead than follow, so the boss is a role they are well suited for.

Their incredible vision allows them to see the necessary improvements needed for any system to function better, and a leadership role will give them the power they desire to take a company or organization forward.

Weaknesses

Since on top is where they would rather be, Green bosses must be careful not to end up there alone with no one following. They have great ideas, but their strength is not in their people skills. They need to have someone on their team who has the ability to motivate and inspire others. Green-Blues will have more skills in this area. We can't be all things to all people, but we need to be smart enough to recognize this and reach out to those who have strengths that we don't have.

Green bosses also have to be careful not to be too autocratic in their decision-making and allow others to be part of the process.

Golds: Some Tips on How Others Can Relate to Them

Do:

1. Carry through with what you say you're going to do
2. Show them the practicality in an idea or a product
3. Be on time
4. Say "thank you" and reciprocate when you receive gifts from them
5. Remember their birthdays
6. Acknowledge them when they do something well
7. Give them time to plan things.

Don't:

1. Expect them to be spontaneous
2. Ask them to spend their money frivolously
3. Force them to take risks
4. Use profane language around them
5. Demand too much immediate change
6. Expect them to challenge the law or any established rules
7. Insist they make decisions without all the facts.

The Kinds of Gifts to Give Golds

(something practical)

a calendar
a clock
a TV
a needed household appliance
a gift certificate to a favorite store
china
silver
a retirement and financial planning seminar
a time management system
"how to" books
a conservative suit
a cookbook or recipe book
a Cross pen/pencil set
cultured pearl earrings
attractive picture frames
money
a sentimental card
a sewing machine
photos of loved ones
a telephone book cover
a decorated tissue box cover
a roll of postage stamps

Famous Gold Personalities:

Role models are those people who we resonate with because of shared values. We relate to others who are like us. The following list contains famous personalities which Golds have identified as people they relate to.

Andrew Johnson*
Benjamin Harrison*
Billy Graham
Calvin Coolidge*

Connie Chung
Dan Rather
David Brinkley
George Bush
Gerald Ford
Grover Cleveland*
Harry Truman*
Henry Ford
J. Edgar Hoover
James Buchanan*
James Monroe*
James Polk *
Jerry Falwell
John McLaughlin
John Tyler*
Julia Child
Margaret Thatcher
Millard Fillmore*
Nancy Reagan
Newt Gingrich
Pat Buchanan
Pat Robertson
Pete Wilson
Phil Gramm
Queen Elizabeth
Robert Dole
Rush Limbaugh
Rutherford B. Hayes*
Walter Cronkite
William H. Harrison*
William McKinley*
William Taft*
Winston Churchill
Woodrow Wilson*

* These Presidents were identified as having the Gold (Gruarian SJ) personality in the book *Presidential Temperament* by David Keirsey and Ray Choinier.

Understanding the strengths and weaknesses of the Gold boss

Strengths

Gold bosses' real strength is in getting things done. The fact that they like to be responsible drives them to do what needs to be done in any situation. The role as boss in a business setting is a natural thing for most Golds with the exception of Gold-Blues, who are more like Blues and may not like this role as much as other Golds. Gold bosses' loyalty is to their companies and they will see to it that deadlines are met, people are doing their jobs, and rules are followed. These are part of any boss's job but Golds do these things naturally and will tend to make sure everybody else does as well.

Weaknesses

Gold bosses must be careful not to be overly loyal to the company and disregard the needs of individuals. People need to feel they are the most important resource of any company and Gold bosses will need to find a balance. Also these bosses have a tendency to be perfectionists, which can be discouraging to others. They'll need to learn to be considerate of those who don't do things exactly the way they would like them done.

Oranges: Some Tips on How Others Can Relate to Them

Do:
1. Be upbeat around them
2. Appreciate their jokes and playful nature
3. Allow them to be independent
4. Provide some structure for them yet be flexible
5. Respect their need to stay busy doing things

6. Understand their ability to do several things at the same time
7. Have fun with them.

Don't
1. Be intimidated by their energy
2. Expect to stay depressed in their presence
3. Be surprised at their changeable nature
4. Force them to be too serious about life
5. Demand that they stick to a strict schedule
6. Write them off as flakes because of their lightheartedness
7. Start a fight with them unless you intend to fight.

The Kind of Gifts to Give Oranges

(something fun)
a trip
state-of-the-art stereo equipment
an expensive dinner
a day at Disneyland or Disneyworld
a ticket to a game show
a big screen TV
a surprise party
a subscription to *Playboy* or *Playgirl* magazine
a skiing trip
an evening at the Comedy Store
a favorite music album
favorite tools
a ticket to a favorite ball game or concert
a shower massager
exercise equipment
money
a humorous card
a motorcycle
a body massage
luggage

a restaurant gift certificate
a health spa membership
sports items such as tennis racket, golf clubs, a volleyball
guitar lessons
karate lessons
dancing lessons
a gym bag

Famous Orange Personalities

Role models are those people whom we resonate with because of shared values. We relate to others who are like us. The following list contains famous personalities which Oranges have identified as people they relate to.

Anita Baker
Arsenio Hall
Bart Simpson
Bill Clinton
Burt Reynolds
Cher
Desi Arnaz
Diana Ross
Donald Trump
Eddie Murphy
Elvis Presley
Florence Griffith-Joyner
Franklin D. Roosevelt
Goldie Hawn
Janet Jackson
Joan Rivers
Les Brown
Lucille Ball
Madonna
Magic Johnson
Marilyn Monroe
Mark Twain

Mark Victor Hansen
Matt Groening
Mohammed Ali
Richard Pryor
Ronald Reagan
Roseanne
Sammy Davis Jr.
Sylvester Stallone
Ted Kennedy
Theodore Roosevelt
Tom Cruise
Willard Scott

Understanding the Strengths and Weakness of the Orange Boss

Strengths

Since Orange bosses have a strong resistance to too much structure and too many restrictions, they will not be likely to impose these on their workers. The tone they set in the office will create a more relaxed atmosphere where others feel free to laugh and be sociable on the job. But when things do go wrong they will have no problem putting out fires. Confrontation does not intimidate them.

Weaknesses

Orange bosses need to be careful about starting things without paying attention to follow-through and implementation. Others are better at filling in the details to complete projects, so they must allow them to do so.

Appendix B:

Identifying Your True Colors

Step I: Visualize Yourself.

As you read the following passages, look closely at the corresponding color illustrations on the front of each Character Card. Do not yet turn over the cards.

Green: "I have this new program for making the organization run like clockwork. Thirty-five years of research, coupled with a computerized network of state-of-the-art equipment will give us a head start on the new program..." (New ideas, new technology.)

Blue: "I realize that good material is very necessary to start, but we have to consider the personnel. They have their rights too, you know. After all, Harry's feelings should be considered before starting this program — or anything, for that matter..." (Feeling, compassionate, adaptable.)

Orange: "As I see it, the world belongs to those who take action, and 'action' is my middle name! By the time the organizers have it organized, I'll have it done and be ready for something new. So, whattaya say? Let's start now..." (Impulsive, immediate, independent.)

Gold: "I think a clear-cut down-to-business mode will get us to the bottom line here. After all, this institution has been here longer than the rest of us and it is our responsibility to see that promises are kept and that the program runs smoothly..." (Responsible, practical, need to belong.)

Now that you are familiar with at least a few of the color group characteristics, rank the cards from the one that is most like you to the one that is least like you.

Step 2: Read About Yourself.

Now, turn over the Character Cards and read the back of each. Arrange them again from the one most like you to the one least like you. Score them in the boxes below using a (4) for the most like you, a (3) second, a (2) third, and a (1) for the one least like you.

Step 3: Describe Yourself.

With the boxes below are groups of words in rows. Score each group of words giving yourself (4) for the most like you, (3) for the second, (2) for the third, and (1) for the least like you. (Score words across)

Orange	Gold	Blue	Green
☐	☐	☐	☐
Active / Opportunistic / Spontaneous	Parental / Traditional / Responsible	Authentic / Harmonious / Compassionate	Versatile / Inventive / Competent
☐	☐	☐	☐
Competitive / Impetuous / Impactful	Practical / Sensible / Dependable	Unique / Empathetic / Communicative	Curious / Conceptual / Knowledgeable
☐	☐	☐	☐
Realistic / Open-minded / Adventuresome	Loyal / Conservative / Organized	Devoted / Warm / Poetic	Theoretical / Seeking / Ingenious
☐	☐	☐	☐
Daring / Impulsive / Fun	Concerned / Procedural / Cooperative	Tender / Inspirational / Dramatic	Determined / Complex / Composed
☐	☐	☐	☐
Exciting / Courageous / Skillful	Orderly / Conventional / Caring	Vivacious / Affectionate / Sympathetic	Philosophical / Principled / Rational
☐	☐	☐	☐
Total Orange	Total Gold	Total Blue	Total Green

Step 4: Identify Your True Colors.

Now total the columns, *including the card points.* Your highest score indicates your primary, or brightest, color; the lowest score represents the color that is least like you.

Record your color Spectrum on the next page

Scoring Your True Colors

Now that you have sorted your Character Cards and discovered and read about yourself, have you identified your color spectrum?

Write your color spectrum below. If you are unable to do so at this point, try repeating the process for additional clarity. Or, you may wish to ask people who know you well just how they see you.

My Brightest Color

_____

The color of your highest total

My Brightest Color Is Shaded with

_____

The color of your second highest total

and

_____

Color of your second lowest total

with

_____

A pale color of your lowest total

Bibliography

Anderson, N. *Work With Passion.* New York: Carroll and Graf
Publishers, Inc., 1984.

Bennett, H. Z. and S. J. Sparrow. *Follow Your Bliss.* New York:
Avon Books, 1990.

Berens, Linda V., Cooper, Sue A. and Giovanni, Louise
Introduction to Temperament. Huntington Beach, California;
1986, First Edition p.4.

Bolt, L.G. *Zen and the Art of Making a Living.* New York:
Arkana, 1991.

Bolles, R.N. *How to Find Your Mission in Life.* Berkeley, CA:
Ten Speed Press, 1991.

— *What Color Is Your Parachute?* Berkeley, CA: Ten Speed
Press, 1997.

Branden, N. *Honoring the Self.* New York: Bantam, 1988.

— *How To Raise Your Self-Esteem.* New York: Bantam, 1987.

— *The Psychology of Self-Esteem.* Los Angeles: Nash
Publishing, 1969.

California Task Force to Promote Self-esteem and Personal and
Social Responsibility. *Toward a State of Esteem.* California
State Department of Education, 1990.

Canfield, J. and H. Wells. *100 Ways to Enhance Self-Concept in
the Classroom.* Englewood Cliffs: Prentice-Hall, 1976.

Choinier, R. and D. Keirsey. *Presidential Temperament.* Del
Mar: Prometheus Nemesis Book Company, 1992.

Chopra, D. *The Seven Spiritual Laws of Success.* San Rafael:
Amber-Allen Publishing, 1994.

Coopersmith, S. *The Antecedents of Self-Esteem.* San Francisco:
Freeman, 1967.

Covey, S. R. *The 7 Habits of Highly Effective People.* New
York: Fireside, 1989.

Edwards, P. and S. Edwards. *Finding Your Perfect Work.* New York: G.P. Putnam's Sons, 1996.

Gawain, S. *Creative Visualization.* Mill Valley: Whatever Publishing, 1978.

Gibran, K. *The Prophet.* New York: Alfred A. Knopf, 1923.

Goleman, D. *Emotional Intelligence.* New York: Bantam, 1995.

Hansen, M.V. *Future Diary.* Newport Beach: Mark Victor Hansen Publishing, 1983.

Haskins, James. *I Have a Dream.* Brookfield, CT: Milbrook Press, 1992.

Hill, N. *Think and Grow Rich.* New York: Fawcett Crest, 1960.

Isachsen, O. and L. V. Berens. *Working Together.* Coronado: Neworld Management Press, 1988

Jeffers, S. *Feel the Fear and Do It Anyway.* New York: Fawcett Columbine, 1987.

Jung, C.G. *Psychological Types.* Princeton: Princeton University Press, 1971.

Kalil, C. and D. Lowry. *How to Express Your Natural Skills and Talents in a Career.* Laguna Beach: Communication Companies International, 1989.

Keirsey, D. *Portraits of Temperament.* Del Mar: Gnosology Books Ltd., 1987.

Keirsey, D. and M. Bates. *Please Understand Me.* Del Mar: Gnosology Books Ltd., 1984.

Ketterman, D. *Hitting the Synergy Bullseye.* 1998.

Kroeger, O. and J. M. Thueson. *Type Talk.* New York: Delacorte Press, 1988.

Maslow, A. H. Motivation and Personality. New York: Harper and Row, 1970.

— *Toward a Psychology of Being.* New York: Van Nostrand Reinhold, 1968.

McLaughlin, C. and G. Davidson. *Spiritual Politics.* New York: Ballantine Books, 1994.

Miller, A. *The Drama of the Gifted Child.* New York: Basic Books, 1981.

— *For Your Own Good.* New York: The Noonday Press, 1983.

Mother Teresa. *My Life for the Poor.* South Yarmouth, MO: J. Curley and Associates, 1985.

Myers, I. *Manual: The Myers-Briggs Type Indicator.* Palo Alto: Consulting Psychologists, 1962.

— *Dictionary of Occupational Titles.* Washington, DC: Employment and Training, U.S. Department of Labor, 1992.

— *Occupational Outlook Handbook.* Washington, DC: U.S. Department of Labor, Bureau of Labor Statistics, 1996-97.

Myers, I. B. and P. B. Myers. *Gifts Differing.* Palo Alto: Consulting Psychologists Press, Inc., 1980.

Satir, V. *The New Peoplemaking.* Palo Alto: Science and Behavior Books, 1988.

— *Peoplemaking.* Palo Alto: Science and Behavior Books, 1972.

Sinetar, M. *Do What You Love, The Money Will Follow.* New York: Dell Publishing, 1987.

Steinem, Gloria. *Revolution from Within.* Boston: Little, Brown and Company, 1992.

Steiner, C. M. *Scripts People Live.* New York: Grove Press, Inc., 1974.

Stephan, N. *Fulfill Your Soul's Purpose.* Walpole: Stillpoint Publishing, 1994.

Taylor, A. *Healing Hands.* Boston: Charles E. Tuttle Company, 1992.

Tieger, P. D. and B. Barron-Tieger. *Do What You Are.* Boston: Little, Brown and Company, 1992.

Zukav, G. *The Seat of the Soul.* New York: Fireside, 1989.

About *True Colors*

Our vision at *True Colors* is to foster positive, healthy, productive communities whose success flows from the natural dedication of each respected person. Our powerful, customized, "edutainment" workshops, training sessions, books, workbooks, videos, live shows, and events have empowered millions of people during the past twenty years and helped to realize this dream.

True Colors "edutainment" always begins with an easy, fun, "Who-am-I?" color card game that keys people to the four basic character traits that make each of us unique. Through innovative, interactive activities, participants learn to communicate their newly described selves in virtually any personal and professional situation. Our positive, revolutionary approach results in dramatically improved and successful lives.

To order additional sets of cards or to request more information about *True Colors* services and products, and instructional material on classroom applications of the *True Colors* process:

True Colors Inc.
3605 W. MacArthur Blvd. #702
Santa Ana, CA 92704

Telephone: 800-422-4686
or 714-437-5426
Fax: 866-374-8958
E-mail: info@true-colors.com

About the Author

For the last twenty-five years, Carolyn Kalil, M.A., has counseled more than 20,000 students of all ages to help them find purpose in their lives. She discovered the *True Colors* System in 1988, which brought about profound changes in her life. In her work at one of California's largest community colleges, Carolyn Kalil has been using the *True Colors* System — a deceptively simple method — with her students so that they, too, can discover their natural talents and strengths. She found the results so rewarding that she co-authored with Don Lowry, founder of *True Colors,* the popular workbook *How to Express your Natural Skills and Talents in a Career.*

As a well-known, sought-after counseling expert, the author lectures on her favorite subject — Follow Your True Colors to the Work You Love — and has facilitated workshops and seminars to thousands of people in the United States and abroad.

Carolyn Kalil has a B.A. degree in elementary education and earned her M.A. in counseling from Ohio State University. She lives with her husband in southern California.

‹ ‹ ‹ › › ›

Carolyn wants to hear from you. If this book improves your life in any way, please write to her and tell her your story.

Carolyn Kalil
E-mail: CKalil@TrueColorsCareer.com
Web site: www.truecolorscareer.com

To order additional copies of

Follow Your True Colors
to the Work You Love

Book: $19.95   Shipping/Handling: $8.95

Contact: **True Colors, Inc. Publishing**
3605 W. MacArthur Blvd, #702
Santa Ana, CA 92704
Phone: 1-800-422-4686
Phone: 714-437-5426
Fax: 866-374-8958
E-mail: info@true-colors.com
www.true-colors.com

ORANGE

I act on a moment's notice.

Witty · Charming · Spontaneous

I consider life as a game, here and now.

Impulsive · Generous · Impactful

I need fun, variety, stimulation, and excitement.

Optimistic · Eager · Courageous

I value skill, resourcefulness, and freedom.

Physical · Immediate · Fraternal

I am a natural trouble-shooter, a performer, and a competitor.

At work or in school, I need to be "hands on"; I like to play games, to compete, and to perform. I enjoy flexibility, changes of pace, and variety; I have difficulty with routine and structure. My favorite subjects are music, art, theater, and crafts. I often excel in sports. I like solving problems in active ways and negotiating for what I want. I can be direct and like immediate results.

With friends, planning ahead bores me because I never know what I want to do until the moment arrives. I like to excite my friends with new and different things, places to go, and romantic moments.

With family, I need a lot of space and freedom. I want everyone to have fun. It is hard for me to follow rules, and I feel we should all just enjoy one another.

1.800.422.4686 · www.true-colors.com

GREEN

I seek knowledge and understanding.

Analytical · Global · Conceptual

I live life by my own standard.

Cool · Calm · Collected

I need explanations and answers.

Inventive · Logical · Perfectionistic

I value intelligence, insight, integrity, and justice.

Abstract · Hypothetical · Investigative

I am a natural non-conformist, a visionary, and a problem solver.

At work or in school, I work best by myself. I like to focus on my ideas until my desire for understanding is satisfied. I am easily bored if the subject holds no interest to me. Sometimes, it is hard for me to set priorities because so many things are of interest.

With friends, I may seem reserved. Although my thoughts and feelings run deep, I am uneasy with frequent displays of emotion. I enjoy people who are interesting and of high integrity.

With family, I am probably seen as a loner because I like a lot of private time to think. Sometimes, I find family activities boring and have difficulty following family rules that don't make sense to me. I show love by spending time with my family and sharing ideas and interests.

1.800.422.4686 · www.true-colors.com